The Long Way Around

"Who Is Josiephine DéLight?"

Receive The Truth!
Act On It!
And
See The Change!

Veronica L. Bea

The Long Way Around

"Who Is Josiephine DéLight?"

Receive The Truth!
Act On It!
And
See The Change!

Veronica L. Bea

Copyright © 2004 • All Rights Reserved
No part of this manuscript may be reproduced, stored in a retrieval system, or transmitted in any form or by any means- without the written permission of the author. The only exception is brief quotations in printed reviews. All Scripture quotations are taken from the King James Version of the Bible unless otherwise indicted.

PUBLISHED BY:
BRENTWOOD CHRISTIAN PRESS
4000 BEALLWOOD AVENUE
COLUMBUS, GEORGIA 31904

About this book

The story of a woman's journey...wife...mother...the product of rejection and the cost...a doormat for seventeen years...Striving to please by any means necessary...Who am I...Lost and found...Home at last...I Saw the Light...Changed...Happy at Last...I Took *The Long Way Around.*

Dedicated To:

To those who have been divinely placed in my life for such a time as this. To all the ones who encouraged and applauded our efforts to bring this project forth. To my wonderful husband Charles who so graciously allowed us to deliver this baby. To our sons of wealth and favor from the Lord, Tony and Travis, my Dear Mom, my sister Borah and Pooch. To those that listened and laughed with us along the way. You know who you are. To those who played parts in the play of, "The Long Way Around." Skeet, Kim and Nois, etc. thanks.

Diamond thanks for your response to, "The Long Way Around Devotional." I never shall forget it. A special thanks to Vikki E. Freeman who worked endless hours typing and preparing this manuscript. Thanks for your belief in the purpose of this project!

To those who taught us to listen to God along the way, your prayers, encouraging words, taking the times out from your busy scheduled to minister to us the word of the Lord.

To the chosen people who have allowed us to pastor them at "The Hand of God Ministries," you light up, "The Lord's House!" Thank you for your prayers! Tom, Hallie and Rose thanks for all your help! Many thanks Gloria.

"General Washington Jr. who sits with Jesus in heavenly places we are still feasting on what you left behind. "Thanks Daddy!"

To YOU the reader! We pray God's blessings upon you in Jesus mighty name!!!

We dedicate this work back to you dearest Lord. We know that you will take the foolish things to confind the wise.

AMEN

"And thou shalt remember all the way which the LORD thy God led thee these forty years in the wilderness, to humble thee, and to prove thee, to know what was in thine heart, whether thou wouldest keep his commandments, or no.

And he humbled thee, and suffered thee to hunger, and fed thee with manna, which thou knewest not, neither did thy fathers know; that he might make thee know that man doth not live by bread only, but by every word that proceedeth out of the mouth of the LORD doth man live.

Thy raiment waxed not old upon thee, neither did thy foot swell, these forty years.

Thou shalt also consider in thine heart, that, as a man chasteneth his son, so the LORD thy God chasteneth thee.

Therefore thou shalt keep the commandments of the LORD thy God, to walk in his ways, and to fear him."

Deuteronomy 8:2-6

FOREWORD

By Vikki E. Freeman, D.Min.,M.C.Ed.

I welcome the opportunity and I find it a privilege and an honor. I take great pleasure in writing the forward for this life changing, mind altering, spiritual enhancing novel. My relationship with Veronica L. Bea extends over a decade and a half and I have come to know and respect her as my friend. There are not very many books that I have in my repertoire that have remotely effected my life like the story of *Josiephine DéLight in the Long Way Around.*

The story of *Josiephine* and *Jack DéLight* will warm your heart. You will surely feel every human emotion that God has given to mankind. It will make you laugh! It will make you cry! It will make you angry! It will make you think as *Josiephine* recoils her life story.

Josiephine differs in no way from you and I. She was a woman like most ordinary women that have experienced dramatic and painful things in their lives. It's how we come out of those experiences that brings about defining moments in our lives.

In the novel, *The Long Way Around* the writer shares with us how Josiephine suffered many things but did not allow herself to remain stuck in any of life's perplexing impasses. As I was preparing the manuscript for this novel I was suffering from what I call *"Sudden Stuck Syndrome."* This is not a psychological diagnosis by a long shot. *"Sudden Stuck Syndrome" is* what I call "when a person finds themselves left in the lurch: stuck in a condition or pattern due to life's devastating situations." Some of us if not all of us, at one time or another, have found ourselves in mind-boggling dilemmas.

It is situations like these that the writer shares with us patterns and other revelations that one can apply to any given situation as she speaks to us through the life of *Josiephine DéLight.* Sometimes the Lord will take you the *The Long Way Around* through the wilderness and He will use uncomfortable circumstances according to His divine Will to propel you forward into His divine plan and purpose. This process will ultimately produce resounding character within us.

This awe-inspiring allegory of faith, hope and encouragement will affirm that there is a plan and purpose for your life. It will affirm that even the casualties of your life experiences can't stop what God has in store for you.

As society and Christendom are still defining and redefining the role of womanhood there is still a vast degree of expectation and fulfillment that we as women have that, has not yet been accomplished neither achieved. For we as women have plateaus and zeniths in God to reach.

Pastor Veronica L. Bea accepted the task to write this guidebook in the form of a novel for women who have suffered doubt, disbelief, disappointment, disillusionment, abandonment and fear. She offers you strength, courage and grace and the help of the Lord's wisdom through the pages of this book. As you accept the challenge to move from your yesterday into your future you will find yourself moving from mediocre to excellent! From ordinary to extraordinary!

THE LONG WAY AROUND

To Teach You

Humility

Spirituality

And Faith

Table of Contents

Chapter		Page
1	The Serving Wife	11
2	Beyond the Call of Duty	15
3	Sinking Ship	19
4	What's Going on	21
5	Out of The Past	26
6	Looking For Peace	29
7	How Can This Be	33
8	The Light	38
9	Changed	42
10	Shocked	45
11	Starting over	49
12	Action	52
13	Too Late	55
14	The Transformation	60
15	Vision	64
16	The Messenger of Love	67
17	The Next Level	70
18	It Came To Pass	73
19	The Same Pattern	76
20	Morning Prayer	79
21	Peace is Contagious	81
22	Smashed to Recovery	84
23	The Manifestation	87
24	The Long Way Around	89

1

The Serving Wife

My name is Josiephine De´Light. For as long as I can remember I never felt wanted or loved by my parents. I didn't come from a poor home. There was always food to eat and clothes to put on. But I never knew what it was to experience real love. I had been rejected all my life. I never seem to fit in. I have two sisters and brothers and yet I had no relationship with them. Perhaps because I am the youngest my parents were tired or disillusioned with life by the time I was born, so I left home as soon as I graduated from high school.

From then on I drifted from one job to another and by the time I was twenty-one I married the first person that asked me to marry him. Surely, this meant I was loved because someone wanted me to spend my life with them. How good it felt to be wanted. My husband was the kind who looked to me for his daily care. Even though he worked each day, how wonderful it felt to be needed. When my husband wanted to look at television, he asked me to turn on the television. When he wanted something special from the store, he asked me to run and get it for him. When he wanted a snack before dinner or after dinner he asked me to get it for him. When he needed his shoes shined, he wanted me to shine them.

By the way my husband's name is Jack. Jack always made me feel so special. He would always tell his friends that he had the best wife in the whole world. When my husband went out of town for special meetings he only had to call home and say pack my bags and I had them already when he got home. Of course when he got back I was only too happy to unpack his bags and wash and iron his clothes and take the necessary things to the cleaners. There were also those special times when he wanted me to massage his back and I was only too glad to do it. I loved being wanted and needed. After being married for three years our first child came along and what a happy time this was. I painted the baby's room a combination of pink and blue with some yellow. My husband was so proud of me. Later on, I did the entire baby's shopping by myself. My husband told his friends how special I was, and even showed them the baby clothes that I picked out.

I don't know when my girlfriends stopped coming to our home to visit as often. However this didn't dampen my spirit because this meant that I had more time to do things for Jack. Oh how I so wanted to please him. I kept his bowling ball sparkling for him and he would come home and share with me how well he bowled. He didn't want me to bowl because he was afraid that I would hurt myself and he couldn't bare the thought of that. I kept his golf clubs clean also and Jack would always tell me how the other husbands envied him because he had the best wife in town. Jack was so thoughtful not wanting me to play golf because I would be exposed to too much sun. I loved the times when we would sit and watch his favorite movies. or when he needed me to sit quietly while he let off steam because of someone who made him mad on that particular day.

By now I was eight months pregnant and had to go to the doctor more frequently. I had gained quite a bit of weight and the doctor was concerned. It was a little icy outside but I felt such a warm satisfaction as I left my husband sitting on the couch with his feet up and a cup of his favorite hot chocolate in his hand. He told his friends if Josiephine didn't make the hot chocolate he didn't want any part of it. As I walked carefully down our driveway I pulled my coat tight around me for I knew that I would have a few minutes to wait before the bus came. I never did learn to drive. I was learning to when I first met Jack. Jack said don't even think about driving that he was my knight in shining armour. In the beginning he used to take me everywhere I needed to go. Then I began to take the bus because he worked hard and needed his rest. I could have called a cab but Jack encouraged me to save money for our future as much as possible, Christmas was coming up and

I wanted to get Jack something special. He loved gifts. He was like a little boy at Christmas time anxious to see all the nice things that I sacrificed and saved so I could make this day special for him.

We were not church going people but on the first Sunday of each year we would go together. I always felt so proud to walk in with my husband. And whenever the preacher said wives were to submit to their husbands I felt so proud of myself. My husband would look at me at those times and give me a radiant smile. Oh how I loved to see that man smile. The baby was due any day now, and I saved money for a cab just in case Jack wasn't home I could get to the hospital. Jack had a lot of special meetings he was involved in. He worked on different committees and did fund raising for a lot of good causes. Therefore it could be a night when he wasn't available to take me to the hospital. What a pillar he was in the community. If anyone needed assistance he always tried to help them. "Ouch!" It's time for me to call a cab to the hospital. The pains were coming closer together now. I arrived at the hospital right on time. Five minutes later my water broke and it wasn't long thereafter that the baby came. A little boy, looking just like his dad. Oh how proud Jack was when he saw his son for the very first time. Jack looked at me in that special way and said, "Honey I promise to teach our son how to be a man. Honey guess what? I can't wait to teach him how to bowl and play golf."

For the first time in years I thought about my parents. I moved from my hometown and never looked back. Now looking at this tiny infant I wondered how my mother felt when she first looked at me. Right then I made a vow that I would never reject my child. That I would do all I could to let him know that he was wanted and loved. I decided right then to drop a card in the mail announcing the birth of our son. My life was so complete that I felt no need to keep in contact with my family. However I would go so far as to send a picture that my brothers and sisters could see my little knight in shining armour.

Coming out of a deep sleep I felt someone shaking me gently and lovingly saying, "Honey, the baby is crying." It was time to get a bottle for Lil' Jack Jr. I was so tired and sleepy, but I managed to pull myself together and saw that it was 2:00 a.m. Perhaps if I hurried and fed him he would stay in that sleep mode and I could sleep before his 5:00 a.m. feeding. Lil' Jack thought nothing of waking up at odd hours and demanding to be fed.

It's 6:00 a.m. and it seems like I just laid down. I have to make Jack's favorite breakfast because this is Friday and after work he has a bowling tournament. He always feels better bowling after a hearty breakfast. Bacon, eggs, grits, pancakes, sausage-gravy, and fresh baked cinnamon buns. Oh how Jack loved my fresh baked cinnamon buns. Perhaps because he was given up for adoption and raised in one foster home after another. He never knew what it was to have a hot breakfast. I made it a daily affair to always grind up fresh coffee beans for his coffee and he loved rich cream poured in. He would eat heartily telling me his plans for that day. He checked his watch and jumped up, kissed my cheek and said "Honey don't forget to take my clothes to the cleaners." That meant I would have to grab the baby and take the bus across town to his favorite cleaners. It would have been great to call in the sitter for the baby. The sitter sometimes kept Lil' Jack for special occasions like celebrating Jack's birthday out or if he needed me to help him at one of his fund raising functions. Why waste money when it's not necessary? oh! Almost missed the bus. It was raining so hard that I stayed in as long as possible waiting for the rain to slack off. Then forgot Jack's favorite suit and had to go back for it. Jack had a wonderful wardrobe. We used our money wisely to spend most of our clothing allowance on Jack's wardrobe because he was before the public more than I. Jack said it would benefit our future if he always dressed for success. He paid special attention to the latest styles. Also he had a membership at the athletic club and went three times a week at least. He wanted me to see him looking his best.

Back home now and I got to hurry and get supper on. Jack loved a hot dinner after a evening of bowling and if it wasn't hot he would lovingly ask me to reheat it for him. But reheating it would cause him to be late watching his favorite game show.

2

Beyond the Call of Duty

Sitting here at the table looking out the window thinking I really needed to get the grass cut and trimmed before Jack got back from his trip this weekend. Perhaps I should wait until later because Lil' Jack might wake up while I am cutting the grass. I decided to sit back and try that new flavored ice cream that Jack loved so much; before I realized it, I had eaten half the carton. I can't keep this up. We only have been married a little over four years. Lil' Jack is now six months old and I have gained sixty pounds. This is not fair to Jack. When I met Jack I was a cool 5'4" and weighed 110 pounds. I'll have to stop eating all those rich desserts. Jack loves for me to keep plenty of bakery goods around the house in case he gets a taste for something sweet. This weekend I'm going to make his favorite, pecan pies with whip cream on top. Jack eats just a little and the next day he wants me to make him something else special. Usually while he is at work I eat the leftovers. Jack tells his friends I am the best cook in town.

Jack brought me a big fancy grill for special cookouts when he would invite his friends over to eat, sometimes with a moment's notice. Jack loved the fact that I could always come up with a feast without even having to go to the grocery store. I always kept the freezer packed with food in case Jack wanted us to do something special. Usually Jack would sit and watch his favorite television show while I cleaned up. No matter how long it took Jack would wait to thank me for being so special. Jack loved the fact that I did not ever serve his food on paper plates or use plastic cups or utensils.

Lil' Jack is growing and so full of energy. He reminds me so much of his dad and has that same smile that his dad has. He is a chip off the old block. His room is cluttered with toys. Jack gets such a joy in buying him toys even though he is too young to play with most of them. One day he came home with a bowling ball for Lil' Jack and I said, "Honey it will be years before he can even pick up that ball." I was thinking about all this money that was lying around the house in toys when Jack needed a new brown winter coat. He already had a black, tan, navy, charcoal, multi-tweed and creamy white winter coat, but no brown, I was a little concern because he loved to dress for success and our future. Also he needed a creamy white brim hat to go with that creamy white coat. On Saturday perhaps I'll run over to L.A.P. & Freedom Hat Store and pick up the best hat in the store for Jack. I usually loved going to that store. It is owned by two sisters and they are always full of laughter. I feel better when I go into that store. I always leave with feeling a sense of peace. Now that I think about it I can't wait to get there. The shop is interesting. It is decorated in a unique way and they must love flowers. But there seem to be something else hanging in the air and I don't understand it. Usually on cold days they have hot coffee. There is a freedom in that shop that makes you feel at home. Lil' Jack is usually on his best behavior while we are there and I am sure he loves the attention the sisters give him.

  The next day I set out early so that I could have plenty of time to linger in the store. I also knew that there were cozy little areas in the shop where I could sit and drink coffee if I desired. When I got to the shop the sisters greeted me warmly and said when I needed help to let them know. They were not the type to breathe down your neck. I took off Lil' Jack's hat and coat and sat him on the large size purple and turquoise throw rug in this one particular sitting area that I like the best. I sat back on this lovely charcoal gray couch with the love seat to match. Also, the set had the cutest little throw pillows with charcoal gray, purple and turquoise circles on them. The kind that men wouldn't be afraid of. The shop was well balanced in its decor. They catered to both men and women. Jack even loved to go there when he had time to shop for his own hats. They have the greatest variety of men and women hats in the city. People come from different cities just to shop at L.A.P. &

Freedom. When you wanted something special you could go there and get it. They do hands on decorating in the shop. I liked to stand around and watch. Once Jack needed a fancy hat that would go with a gold sparkly tie and handkerchief and black suit. They put just a hint of gold thread around the brim of a black hat and people are still calling to see where Jack got that hat from. As I sat quietly I noticed all the different types of baskets with different items for sale in them. The shop smelled of frankincense and myrrh. There were all kinds of interesting pictures and novelty items around. In the ceiling it was covered with flowers, birds, hats and other interesting things. There was the sound of a waterfall, but I have never seen a fountain in the shop. The window was so pretty. I love to ride pass just to see the window. It feels so peaceful here. What's wrong with me, I have a beautiful home, wonderful husband, a beautiful healthy baby; yet, as I sit here I don't want to leave and go home. Business is certainly excellent here, people are in and out constantly and yet there is such a peace in the air." Josiephine De´Light, girl what is wrong with you today?" Life couldn't be better. Jack just got a promotion on the job making a lot more money, which also means he has to travel more. However Jack loves traveling and meeting new people; so what am I thinking about?

While there I noticed the fancy women's hats and thought how pretty but where would I ever wear one? They had a hat that I knew Jack would love and I quickly brought it. I talked with one of the sisters and she asked me how was I doing? I told her I was busy, busy. There seem to be so much to do. My how the time flies. I looked at my watch and told her that I had to run. I wanted to make sure that I got the clothes washed and dried before Jack got home. Jack loved the house to be sparkling and I tried to keep it that way. Which reminds me the corners of the kitchen floor needed scrubbing. That meant that I would have to stop at the store and pick up a hard toothbrush. The last one was too weak to reach into the cracks and clean sufficiently.

Sitting on the bus I noticed how old and wrinkled my hands were becoming. I saw my reflection in the bus window and I looked twice my age and plus I gained ten more pounds. I thought about how nice it would be to get a manicure. To just sit back and have someone else do my nails instead of me trying to hurry up and do them between Lil' Jack and trying to get dinner cooked. Maybe I'll put aside just a little money and have my nails done in a couple of months. "Come on bus driver," I said to myself as he was talking to someone who had just gotten off the bus. I was in a hurry, I thought about I had promised Jack that I would make him yeast rolls. I could make them and let them rise while I was finishing the laundry. Tomorrow I could do all the ironing after I got back from Lil' Jack's doctor appointment.

"Honey those are the best yeast rolls that I have ever eaten! I was eating in this five star restaurant where all the movie stars go, and honey your yeast rolls would put them to shame. How about I invite the fellows over for a cookout this weekend?" "Jack the weatherman said, it was going to rain." "Honey I'll pick you up a raincoat and you can grill out on that new gas grill that we brought, (with the four burners, the rotisserie for the kabobs, and the refrigerator at the bottom). You'll be fine out there. The fellows and I don't mine eating inside. Honey make some of that special garlic bread, some hot baked beans, corn on the cob, cole slaw and potato salad, and honey, don't forget to marinate the ribs the night before. Make it light on yourself and just make your good old fashion brewed ice cold tea and make a plain pound cake, something simple."

"Josiephine honey, you are putting on quite a bite of weight. I think you better lay off that pound cake today. I want you to stay healthy. By the way Jo, that cook out was great. How do you do it? Josiephine, did you hear me? I said that the cook out was great even though we had to eat inside because of the rain. Honey I won't be home for supper. I got committee meetings tonight." "All right Jack, honey, have a great day." Now what was that music that was playing in the hat store? I'll have to ask those sisters next time I go there.

3

Sinking Ship

Wherever did the years go? Tonight Jack and I are celebrating our seventh wedding anniversary. Jack is allowing me to ride in a taxi on this special occasion to meet him at one of the best restaurants in town. We are dining with four other couples tonight. This is the fifth outfit I have tried on and it is outdated and I can't even fasten it up. My weight is out of control. I can't seem to stop eating no matter how many times I promised myself that I will. Perhaps if Jack were home I would eat less. How can I expect him to be home with me when his job has him constantly on the road? Even when he is in town working he has to spend most of his time in the office. Some nights he sleeps over at the office so he won't come in late and disturb me. Jack has continued to be so thoughtful where I am concerned. Oh my goodness! The taxi will be here in fifteen minutes. Thank goodness that I asked the sitter to come early so Lil' Jack would be taken care of while I got ready. Well back to my old black rubber dress. I'll have to wear it. That is one garment that I can depend on. It will stretch to accommodate my size.

I looked in the mirror and had to admit that I looked more like Jack's mother than I did his wife. How sad, but true. My hair was so outdated so I just twisted it and pinned it up. This will have to do. I promised myself that I would talk to Jack about at least getting my hair done and maybe a manicure. I could see rolls and rolls of fat around my middle and even my face was no longer the same. Makeup couldn't hide the sagging fat around my neck and under my chin. Well, at least I am happily married and my husband really loves me. How lucky I am to be married to someone who really loves me. Jack often tells me that he doesn't know what he would do without me. Oh, I wish I had brought some of the perfume that I saw the other day. The smell was incredible and the price was out of my budget. Plus I was saving to buy Jack something special for our anniversary. After all he is taking me out to dinner tonight and four more couples besides me. It still would have been nice to at least smell good for Jack.

As I stepped into the restaurant I felt out of my league. It was so fancy and all the women were dressed so elegant and looked so beautiful. I asked for my husband and I was led to the table where he was already enjoying himself tremendously. Everyone was laughing and when I got to the table they greeted me politely as I sat next to Jack. I noticed how well groomed each of the women looked and their weight was just right for their frame. Marva was the one that always gave me a warm smile while the others had a look in their eyes that made me feel as if I was under a microscope. I was still determined to enjoy myself. It wasn't often that Jack could pull away from his job to take me out. This place is top of the line. Jack ordered for me. He ordered me the liver and rice, the house special and a super salad. I noticed the others had lobster right along with Jack. Also they drank bottles of the finest wine. I drank very little. Somehow I couldn't get in the flow of enjoying myself. The conversation was centered around their jobs, their business adventures, their latest investments, or what was going on in our world. I was so busy with my life and the care of my family that I hardly remembered who was the President of our country. Needless to say who was running for office. I didn't even have a clue. I spent my free time when I had any on the couch in the family room sleep. Lil' Jack was active and demanded my attention even though he was older and soon to be four years old. Maybe when he starts preschool I will have more time to pamper myself.

4

What's Going on

Here I am sitting down and there is so much to do. Clothes to take to the cleaners, the oven has to be cleaned, the floors needs to be buffed and waxed, Lil' Jack's room has to be cleaned and the walls needs some attention. There is the trash that has to be taken outside. The leaves need to be raked. Jack is away on a business trip and will be home in a couple of days and I got to have this place in tiptop shape. Lil' Jack is in school now and will be home at 2:45 p.m., so that doesn't give me much time. I am so glad that he is big enough to walk to school with his friends. He'll come running home to eat and then go right out to play. Hope he doesn't have a lot of homework that I'll have to end up doing. He'll give me that look just like his father does and I'll melt and give in. I keep thinking about that pecan pie that was left from last weekend. I started to freeze it but instead I found myself eating pie all week. Now there is one slice left that keeps calling my name. I got up and went to the refrigerator and took the slice of pie out, warmed it in the microwave and put heavy whipping cream over the top of it and ate every morsel. Somehow eating seems to bring me such a comfort. I wonder why that is?

I looked around the house, which we have only lived in for a year to check and make sure that everything was just the way Jack liked it. Jack may want to have his friends over tonight. In fact that is one of reason that he wanted this particular house so we could entertain on a larger scale. Tomorrow Jack and Lil' Jack will be spending the whole day together. What a wonderful father Jack is. After every business trip he always makes time to spend at least one whole day with Lil' Jack. I took one last look in the mirror on the wall and I didn't recognize the woman in the mirror. I stopped for a moment and just starred at myself. Who am I? I didn't have any shape or form? My figure was totally gone. I couldn't even pretend anymore. I was wearing one size fit all clothing now. This made life easy for me. You just go to the discount-clothing store in the women's department and pick up something that will easily accommodate your size. I didn't like to spend money on myself. These dresses came in handy even if I lost weight I could still wear them. Christmas was coming up and now I had Lil' Jack to surprise with gifts right along with Jack. I was thinking of getting him a couple pairs of those gym shoes that he has been asking for. After all these years I still make it a point to tuck away a little money here and there to make sure that I get the men in my life something special.

    As I climbed the stairs I had to stop and rest along the way. I was getting out of breath a lot these days. I noticed while raking the leaves that I had to stop and rest. It took me two days to get the yard in shape. Now it is time to do it again. Usually I have all the laundry done by now, grocery put away, furniture polished, food on for tonight's dinner. Today I can't seem to get moving fast enough. I'll rest in a moment and get a bite to eat and I'll feel better. While sitting over coffee and eating grilled cheese sandwiches I thought about the visit over at L.A.P and Freedom Hat Store the other day. I stopped in to see the new fall line of hats for men. The shop had that same thing in the air. I can't put a name on it. I know that I don't experience that feeling in all stores. I've been in stores that are more upscale and beautiful, and I don't experience that peace. I guess that's what you call it.

    I sat there in that special section in the store and didn't want to leave. There was music playing in the background and there was a video on the television of a man preaching and he was saying something about "Jesus Loves you." Some how those words seemed to hang in the air as if that man was talking directly to me. I got up to leave after that. The two sisters were both there and I noticed how neat they both looked. Their weight was just the right size. I wonder if they ever had a weight problem. I didn't have the nerve to ask them. It was like another part of me wanted to open up. There seem to be a cry springing up for help. I never had a desire to allow someone to see into me like that. Somehow that made me feel like I was exposing myself and I couldn't explain what brought that on.

Climbing on the bus took great effort. Somehow I was steadily gaining weight. As I sat on the bus I was glad it wasn't crowded. I took up most of the seat and was glad when the bus came to my stop. I took longer to get off and had to rest as I walked toward the house. "Jo, girl you can't sit here all day." But some how I couldn't get moving. Evening came and I was still sitting in the same spot when Jack and Lil' Jack came in. Jack looked around and groceries were still not put away, clothes were unfolded, still in the clothesbasket and the house didn't have that aroma of dinner cooking. Jack and Lil' Jack just looked at me and didn't say a word but just walked away as if I had hurt their feelings. I felt so bad and continued to sit there in that same spot way pass midnight.

The next morning I got up to make Jack and Lil' Jack their favorite breakfast. They both came down stairs together and Jack said for the first time in our married life that he didn't want breakfast and Lil' Jack responded the same way his dad did. After they left I sat down at the table and looked at all that food and I picked up bacon, sausage, eggs and pancakes and began to eat. Later I couldn't help reaching for those fresh baked cinnamon buns and ate them also. I had a doctor's appointment that afternoon and I didn't want to go. But thought I'd better go ahead and keep the appointment. I hurried and put away yesterday's groceries and put a roast on in the oven. Next, I put clothes in the washer and put up yesterday's laundry. I cleaned Lil' Jack's room and wiped off his walls. The lawn needed raking but I didn't have time to do it. I left the house in plenty of time to get to the doctor's office.

I wasn't prepared to see the look of concern on the doctor's face. He asks me how was I feeling and of course I said run down and tired. Then he mentioned that I had gained twenty-one pounds since my last check-up six months ago. I sat and listen as he suggested that I go on a diet. Needless to say that I had already tried dieting a number of times and seemed to gain weight instead of losing it. Never the less I assured the doctor that I would give it another try. He cautioned me about the effects of the weight on my body. He said that I was carrying a load that my body was not built to handle and that I needed to start losing weight now. I passed the nurse on the way out of the office and she said good-bye as if I was just another face in her day. On the way home I wondered how Jack would be when he got home. I never had him to look at me in that way; as if he was seeing me for the very first time and he didn't like what he saw. To make matters worse, Lil' Jack had the same kindred expression. I will make it up to them. I'll make both of their favorite desserts and buy them a little surprise gift on the way home.

I stopped at L.A.P. & Freedom Hat Store and was disappointed that they were closed. I was more disappointed because I would not get to sit in that atmosphere inside the shop, than I was about not getting a gift for Jack and Lil' Jack.

I stood there and stared in the window. I gazed into the shop and I felt a bit of life spring back into me from just gazing into that place.

For the first time I noticed a church next door as I was waiting for the bus. Here was that same color scheme that the shop had. I wonder if the sisters had anything to do with this place. I vaguely sense something tugging at my heart as I looked at this church. It was unusual and there were Christmas trees in the window and inside was decorated in an unusual way. Next, I spotted the flowers in the building and I knew that the two sisters were somehow connected. I had a strange desire to go in. The lights were on and there was even an open sign on the door. Just then the bus pulled up and I really needed to get home and prepare for Jack and Lil' Jack. I'll just have to buy them a gift later. Somehow it didn't seem as important anymore.

Jack came in while Lil' Jack was outside playing and looked in a better mood as he saw the table set and his slippers out. I told him dinner would be on the table in seven minutes and that I would call Lil' Jack in to eat. There was plenty of chatter between Jack and Lil' Jack. They ate their food with great enthusiasm. Later, they had their dessert and left the table talking and enjoying one another. Somehow this didn't bring me the joy that it use to. I felt empty as I looked at my husband and son leave the table. I didn't feel fulfilled even when Jack turned back and said, Great job Josiephine."

5

Out of The Past

As I sat looking out the window at the rain falling. I wondered when was the last time I had time to cry. The rain splashing against the windowpane reminded me of teardrops. As I sat there many thoughts crossed my mind. Where has the time gone? Maybe today was a day for me to reflex on my life. When was the last time that I really laughed? I felt like I was under deep waters and needed to surface. I will be alone this weekend. Jack is out of town for two weeks and Lil' Jack is spending the weekend with his best friend. Lil' Jack isn't little anymore. This year he turned twelve and he's almost as tall as his dad. He runs in and out of the house and I don't really know my own child. All he wants to do is spend time with his friends. Of course, his father believes he should develop relationships with his friends and encourages him to visit their homes.

The ringing of the telephone brought me back to reality. I made it to the telephone on the last ring. I heard a voice that sounded familiar asking for Josiephine De´Light. I said, "This is she." "Jo this is Marlene." I paused for a moment to catch my breath. Now it came to me who that voice belonged to. It was a voice out of the pass, that brought back painful memories. The voice belonged to my oldest sister. "Hello Marlene," I said rather hesitantly.

Marlene said she was coming through town and wanted to stop by to see me. I paused for a moment and told her sure. She informed me that she would be coming in next week and I said that I would be looking forward to her visit. I hung up with an unpleasant feeling in the pit of my stomach. There were a thousand thoughts running through my head. We hadn't talked in years. She was like a stranger to me. I had no idea what to say to her. I would just have to wait and see what she wanted. This meant that my schedule would be interrupted. There were some closets that I was planning on cleaning out on next week. Oh well, I could put it off a few hours.

I wonder what Jack would think about Marlene's visit. Would he be surprised? Would he even remember that I had a sister named Marlene? I wondered also how Lil' Jack would respond? I never spoke to him about any of my family. Maybe he thought my family members were all dead. What a surprise! Old memories kept trying to surface. I remember when I was young and wanted to go with my older sister and her friends, she always told me to get lost. Those were her favorite words she would always hurl at me. The look in her eyes was none to kind. As I grew older I learned not to even ask if I could go with her.

Ring!!! Now Josiephine don't get nervous. I was about to open the door on the past. I wasn't looking forward to this meeting with my sister. However the moment is here. As I walked to the door to greet my sister I felt real tense. I opened the door and on the other side stood a sad middle aged woman who called my name. We just stood there checking each other out. Finally I told her to come in and sit down. I couldn't help but wonder why she came to see me.

I offered her coffee and she said no thanks and looked a little nervous. I asked her how our parents were. She said, "Josiephine that is why I am here. Mom and dad are not doing so good. I have had to move in with them and it is taking a toil on me." As I sat and listened I felt as if I was far away looking at her as an outsider who I never really knew.

We made small talk about my life and she commended me on how beautiful the house was. I told her about Jack and Lil' Jack and that I was sorry they were not here to meet here. As my sister was preparing to leave my home after such a brief visit she turned and said, "Mom and dad often mentions you Josiephine they really would like to see you." I responded briefly that perhaps some day I could pull away to visit them. After a brief hug we parted company. I walked away from the door thinking how old and how bad my sister looked.

I went to the kitchen and caught a glimpse of myself in the mirror. I was startled by what I saw. There stood a woman who looked twice her age and a hundred and twenty-one pounds overweight and I couldn't even see my toes. I looked dreadful and older than my sister. I just stood there and I wondered what had happened to that cute petite girl who said yes to Jack's invitation to be his wife. Where was she? Who is this woman in the mirror starring at me? Why is she crying? Just then the phone rang and it was Jack.

"Josiephine, I won't be home this weekend. I am joining some of the fellows for a bowling tournament. Jo, I need a black and white dress hat. See if L.A.P. & Freedom still has that black fur hat trimmed in the white fur. By the way Josiephine take twenty-five dollars and go to the mall and buy you an outfit. Tell Lil' Jack hello and I'll see you next week." As I hung up I was still numb from what I saw in the mirror. Well, maybe I'll get me a manicure at the mall instead of looking for an outfit.

6

Looking For Peace

As I rose to get up out of the bed this morning I felt a sense of hopelessness. I felt like I was drained. My world seemed to be so small and void of purpose. Usually I rose up with something that I needed to tackle for that day. There was always work to be done. However, today I could not find any sense of fulfillment in getting that work accomplished. The sun was shining through the window and I felt like it was dark outside. The house was quiet but there seem to be a noise coming from every direction. As I moved from room to room I seemed to be still standing still. Is this all there is to life? Where is the peace? Is there joy in the world? I moved to Lil' Jack's room and sat on his bed. As I sat there I tried to take a comfort in the fact that we had such a wonderful son who was the image of his father. Why then does my heart still feel so empty?

As I finished dressing to leave the house to get Jack's hat I didn't even bother to check the mirror to see how I looked. For years the mirror had been my enemy or was it my friend? Telling me truth that I didn't want to face. If I faced the truth that I saw was I not responsible to try and change what I was looking at? I wonder how much could the mirror tell me about myself. My insides felt ugly and disfigured. Can the mirror reflect what was inside me as well as what was outside? Perhaps I'll never know because I didn't want to ever look in the mirror again!

I felt a coldness grip my heart and penned up tears began to freeze. As I headed down the stairs I was reminded how my life seem to be going all down hill. How did I get to such a place? Did I get here step by step? How could I have possibly walked into this pit with my eyes wide open? or was I blinded as I traveled? I don't remember this street. Were there signs along the way that

I refuse to see? The phone rang again and for once I didn't answer it. I wonder if there was a sound along the way that I didn't hear that tried to awaken me. I felt like I was asleep. Looking around at our beautiful home I felt it giving me no warmth. The chairs that I thought were always so inviting to sit in seemed to give a different message this morning. They seem to say, "We are here and we will hold anybody, you are not special to us!"

As I turned to go into the kitchen, a room that always brought me much comfort; I always felt better when I left the kitchen; I opened the refrigerator and saw pie, ice cream, great leftovers, milk, pizzas, and much more; I always kept the refrigerator stocked. Today the contents inside the fridge didn't shout comfort to my soul. Somehow they seem to shout control.

Was it possible that what I thought was comforting to me was really controlling me? Suddenly I slammed the refrigerator shut and went to the sink and got a glass of water. I drank the water slowly as if I was punishing myself in drinking it. I never cared that much for water. How is it that I didn't care for the very thing that was created to keep me alive? Days without water could cause you to lose your life. Did I miss something life giving along the way?

In walking to the bus stop I heard the birds singing and wondered what they were singing about. They seem to be always singing in all kinds of weather. I looked at an apple tree in our beautiful neighborhood and it was dying. I knew some one would call and report it and it would be cut down. I wonder what it felt like to be a tree and be cut down before you could bare fruit.

I got on the bus headed to get Jack another hat. As I so often had done over the years I thought about the last time I was at L.A.P. & Freedom. I had just purchased Jack that black fur hat trimmed in the white fur and was leaving the store and one of the sisters came in the front door and greeted me warmly. I made small talk with her. That day I wasn't myself. The sister told me she would be sure to put my name on the church's prayer list. I sure hope those prayers work. Usually the sisters used the back door to enter the shop. I remember thinking after I talked with her that I was glad she came in the front door. Just that little meeting with her gave me strength somehow. As the bus moved over the bridge to the part of town I was traveling to, I was thinking that I needed a bridge over troubled water. I was so troubled on this day. My life seems to be in shambles.

Jack and Lil' Jack were hardly ever home after seventeen years of marriage. Lil' Jack is thirteen and spends most of his time away from home. He even has gotten to the place where he travels with his dad when he's not in school. I have heard him say, "Hi mom and bye mom" so many times over the years. I don't really know my husband or my son. How can this be? What happened along the way? What was it about me that they were always avoiding my presence?

Jack and I never really had any meaningful conversations. There wasn't any substance to our talks. Afterward nothing came back to nourish me. He left me cold and no doubt I left him the same way. I left nothing to nourish him. When home Jack and Lil' Jack huddled together on the couch and watched television. They seem to enjoy a variety of programs. Educational shows, the news, game shows, sports and old movies seemed to have taken my place. Perhaps I was too busy doing other things. I remember once going in to join them in front of the television and began speaking to them and Jack and Lil' Jack cried out for me to hush at the same time. What was the television serving that I wasn't?

I felt close to tears again and held them back. I couldn't go inside crying. As soon as I opened the door to the hat shop, I felt a peace that I couldn't understand, hit me. What is this? All I did was open the door and walked inside. I could see business was better that ever. There were plenty of customers. The sisters had expanded the shop. They also had new help. Everyone working in this place seemed to have glows on their faces. I sat down at a table in a new sitting area, I went over to get a cup of fresh coffee and cream. As I sat down I loved enjoying the fact that they made the shop so people friendly. This for the first time spoke to me! "Hey Josiephine, somebody here doesn't just want your money or what you can give them. They care about you as a person. They reached out to comfort you." As I sat and looked around I felt peace in the atmosphere. I too could sit here forever. I looked at the sisters and the people they were talking too. I noticed such a peace on them that something on the inside began to eat from the peace that I saw. I felt as if there was another presence with them that was watching me. I found myself wishing that I had this peace.

7

How Can This Be

Maybe I heard wrong! Could this be happening to me? The man that I loved and married for better or worse was standing before me saying that he was leaving! How can this thing be? I thought I did all the right things to please him? I catered to him day and night! I always put his needs above my own and now he stands before me saying, "I'm leaving you." I looked at my husband and said, "Why Jack? What did I do to deserve this?" Jack looked at me and said, "Josiephine, there is no one else, but we have grown apart. Josiephine I don't want to hurt you but I have an apartment in New York City and Lil' Jack wants to live with me." My mouth flew opened and no sound came forth. I just starred in space as the bottom fell out of my world.

"Josiephine, you can stay in the house. I can manage both places for a while, and then later I'll make a decision to sell it or not." "Jack you mean just like that you are leaving and taking Lil' Jack with you?" "Jo, Lil' Jack will be back and forth to see you." "What about you Jack, will you be back?" "Josiephine, I haven't made any plans about the future right now. All I know is that I need space. I thought to myself, "Jack needed space!" I've got to wake up, this must be a dream! I'll wake up in a moment. Yes this is a dream, I'm dreaming! But the pain feels so very real.

Here I sat days later and I can't shake the pain in my heart. Oh how I miss my husband and son and it has only been a few days and I hurt something awful in my heart. I have not been to bed. I have sat for days in this same spot hardly moving, thinking that in a few minutes Jack and Lil' Jack will walk through that door asking what's for dinner. The phone rang, and I jumped to answer it thinking that Jack would be on the other end, saying, that he is coming back to me. But, it wasn't him. I'm still numb and I don't have anyone to talk to. My whole world was about Jack and Lil' Jack. I centered everything around them. I had no girl friends that I could go to and talk about what has happened.

I rejected my family because they rejected me. I felt that my world was complete. Perhaps I could have stood Jack leaving if Lil' Jack had remained with me. Lil' Jack looked uncomfortable for the first time as he said good-bye and left with his father. I should have said that I wanted my son to stay with me. What made me just accept what Jack said? How was I going to live without my husband and son? We kept wine in the house for special occasions. I stood to go and get a glass of wine and something seem to come out of nowhere and say that's not the answer.

The pain in my heart was so real that I knew that the wine would be like trying to cover up the pain. Even food had lost its appeal. I kept thinking that Jack would change his mind. But when I think of the look that was in his eyes, when he told me that he was leaving, I knew that it would take a miracle to bring him back to me. What was I going to do with myself? Jack said that he would continue to pay the bills for a while. However, he let me know that it wouldn't be forever, and that I would have to do something to support myself.

Jack had always handled the money. He would give me just enough to take care of the things we needed in the house. I was able to save a little here and there to buy gifts for Jack and Lil' Jack. I watched the sales papers, and I knew just the right time to go to the supermarket. With coupons I would always come home with some money left over. Also, I took the bus and rarely took a cab. All these things I did so I could give to Jack. I had not one dime saved. For seventeen years I have been a housewife. I never thought about doing anything else. Where do I go from here?

A few days later I needed something from the store and as I waited for the bus I thought about how many times that I have rode this bus to get groceries. There were times that I was loaded down and could hardly carry the bags. Sometimes I'd go back the next day just to pick up something else that was needed. As I walked down the isle of the grocery store I saw one the sisters from the hat shop. I quickly hid myself before she could see me. I felt a sense of peace just seeing this woman. Whenever I went into the hat shop I felt that same peace in the shop. I wasn't expecting to encounter this peace as I pass this woman in the grocery store. I was too ashamed to allow her to see me. She often asked me about Jack and Lil' Jack and would tell me to tell them hello.

I thought about the last time I was at L.A.P. Freedom and talked with both sisters. They invited me to a class at their church called Vision that took place on Thursday evenings. I turned them down and said that I was much too busy. However, this didn't stop them they said that they had a class on Friday evenings call Fragrance. I declined again and they said, well, maybe perhaps, some time in the future I would be able to come. On the way home loaded down with ice cream I thought about those classes again and wondered what they were like.

Here I am at midnight eating ice cream and cookies. "Josiephine you can't keep this up." I knew this wasn't the answer and somehow I couldn't stop eating. I needed something to dull this pain. I had called Jack to speak with Lil' Jack and usually he was at a movie or spending the night out with new friends. This night he was home. He spoke to me so indifferently. Before he hung up he said he wasn't ready to come home and spend the weekend just yet. A lump rose in my throat and I knew even the ice cream couldn't dull this particular pain. I must have fallen off to sleep. Later I woke up to a sound of my name being called. I sat up in bed and realized that I must have been dreaming. It was six o'clock in the morning and I was wide-awake. There was no reason for me to get up. I had no one to cook for, no one to see off to work or school. It was then that I realized that I had nothing else to live for. I felt like jumping off a bridge and ending my life.

Here I was weeks later and the same thoughts keep coming to me that I should end my life. Suddenly the thought came to me. Could I trust death to be a comfort to me? Would death embrace me? Could I find peace there? Was that really the answer? I felt a fear grip my heart. I was uncertain about what I would find on the other side of death. Would I find a friend?

Would there be a peace for me there? I realize that no matter what I had heard about death I had no guarantee that it would end my suffering. Was there life after death? Was there a heaven or hell? Where would I go too? Could I afford to take a chance? This step of death was not reversible. I don't remember hearing of anyone who came back from the dead. Perhaps someone has an answer for me.

The ringing of the phone brought me back to myself. I was surprise to find one of the sisters from the hat shop on the phone inviting me to a prayer meeting at their church.

"Josiephine, you were so on my mind today that I just had to call you." She asked me if I was all right and I found myself telling her about the hell that I have been going through. She said that she knew something was wrong and encouraged me to come out to the prayer meeting. I thanked her for calling and said that I just might come to the prayer service.

As I hung up the phone I wondered how this woman knew to call me at the time I desperately needed someone to talk to. I thought about the last time Jack and I were at church was on the first Sunday of the year three years ago. Somehow a few years ago Jack got so busy that he did not have the time to go anymore and of course I stopped going. The more I thought about the invitation to go to prayer service, I wondered what would it hurt to go.

This could be a way to make the time go by faster in my day. So at seven o'clock I was headed across town to go to a church that I have never been in before. I was warned that it wasn't your average church. I wondered what that meant. Weren't all churches the same?

I got off the bus right in front of the church. The windows were always beautiful. They kept Christmas trees up all year around and somehow it didn't seem out of order. I had always loved looking at the lights. There was an open sign lit up on the door. I opened the door and went in.

When I stepped into the church I didn't know what to expect. The first thing that met me was this peace in the air. It seemed to reach out and surround me. I felt like this peace was embracing me. Next, as I looked around at the unusual place I had a sense of belonging as if I was at home. I was greeted by a nice young girl with long blond hair and was told to relax and grab a cup of coffee if I liked.

There was beautiful music playing. The people seemed very friendly and they had that same peace that I seen on those sisters. As I sat I wondered what all they did in this place. There was a young teenage boy about Lil' Jack's age, and he walked over to the microphone and began to read above the music that was playing softly in the background.

There seemed to be some unseen power filling the room. As he read and began to talk I noticed the people in the room began to get quiet. A moment later someone yelled out "glory." Others began to lift their hands in the air and as they did this, the young teenager cried out, "Praise the Lord?"

The room began to feel like a sauna. It was warm and wet in the atmosphere. I began to feel the first sign of hope touch my heart. It felt like weights were dropping off of me. Suddenly I realized that this young teenager was reading from the Bible. I don't know why this surprised me. Perhaps because, the words coming out of his mouth had such a power with them. I always viewed the Bible as dull and lifeless. I've heard it read before but never had it touched me. When the young boy went to sit down I wanted him to stay there forever, because, it seemed as if someone was pulling chains off of me.

About ten minutes later the youngest sister, who I later found out was the Pastor of this unusual place came out in jeans and tee shirt, wearing an unusual beautiful long gold and blue vest. No doubt she had to slip it over her head because both sides of the vest was open. She said that she had been in worship. I wondered what she meant by that. One thing that was for sure, she was lit up with a presence and power that got off on me. As she stood, she greeted me, and told me that they would be coming together to pray in a moment, I felt a tingling began to go over my body.

8

The Light

  I slept like a baby last night and somehow I knew it was the direct result of that prayer meeting. I don't understand how it happened but when those people gathered around me and began to pray I felt that tingling on my body increase. The Pastor put some oil on each one of us there. She asked me if she could put some oil on me which had a sweet smell to it. I told her go ahead, thinking that I couldn't feel any worse than I did before I came in.

  In fact, since I had been in that place I was feeling so much better. Soon they began to do some unusual singing and they said things like, "We Worship You Lord." I was beginning to feel like raising my hands and I didn't know why. What was happening to me? I didn't really know, and I didn't even care as long as it took that awful pain away that was in my heart, and the heavy feeling away from me.

  All of a sudden some of the people present began to speak in a language that I couldn't understand. Then just as quickly they began to speak where I could understand. They prayed for the President of the United States, leaders of this country, judges, policemen, and the armed forces. When I thought they were through another one would began to pray. Prayers were prayed for the teenagers, prisoners, sick and shut in, some were crying out and others shed tears.

  They seemed to pray as a piece of music being played with an unseen music director in the midst. I felt an unseen hand touch my shoulder. A pure peace was released into me. Then I felt myself fall to the floor. As I lay on the floor in that sweet peace I never wanted to rise again.

  Later as the prayer meeting came to an end someone reached to help me up off the floor. I noticed that look that was on the faces of these people got richer after prayer. I wondered about that as I bided each one good night. Before I left I was invited to please come back again. I said that I would.

That night I didn't go to a bar to get a drink to forget my troubles. I went to a prayer meeting and got drunk and forgot my problems. I smiled as I thought about this and laughed out loud. I couldn't remember the last time that I laughed. I heard birds singing as I rose to get a cup of coffee and a piece of toast and wondered what I would do today. Perhaps I'll check the newspaper and see if there were any jobs that I might be able to do. Somehow I was going to have to earn a living. This didn't seem to frighten me at this moment. I wondered why and again I thought about that prayer meeting. I believe I'll go back this Friday night.

Suddenly, I thought about my husband and son, and sadness tried to press in on my heart. For a moment I almost let it get me down but something within me said, "No I can't live like that." I felt a newfound strength rising up in me. Maybe I'll do something totally different today. I decided to get on the bus and go to the biggest shopping mall in town and just walk.

There were all kinds of people at the mall. Some seemed to be in a big hurry. Some were sitting around and seemed to be enjoying just sitting. There were some overweight like me. Suddenly, I realized that I had some money left from the money Jack sent for the bills. The freezer was still stocked with food so I didn't have buy food. I decided that I would have my nails done. As I sat there having my nails done for the first time in seventeen years, I wondered why I hadn't gotten them done before now. I chose the color polish that I wanted and had medium nails put on my fingers. My nails looked really nice even though my hands were rough and plump.

I decided right then that I would invest in a bottle of hand cream or lotion and keep my hands moisturized each day. I spent years scrubbing and waxing floors for the man I loved and look what I have left, hands that look years older than they should. As I was about to leave the mall I turned around and went back to the store that I just left. I went in and brought some face cream and lipstick. Somehow this made me feel better.

That night before I went to bed I went into the bathroom and washed my face and then put on my new face cream. I spent years-polishing furniture and never thought about my face needing some personal attention. Tomorrow, I'll get my scale out of the closet. I quit weighing myself long ago. It was only when I went to the doctor's office that I had to face the truth of my weight. Now I am going to force myself to step on that scale each week. Perhaps I'll give up drinking sodas for a while. I need to start fighting back. This battle of the bulge was progressive. I needed to at least throw a blow. Here I am at thirty-eight years old an a mere shadow of who I was meant to be.

Truth seemed to be flooding up out of my soul and I was receiving it. As I began to receive the truth, change began to manifest in my life. I looked at my hands and they look so much better. Simply because I receive the truth and I acted on what I saw. A Manicure and the continual putting on of hand cream. Perhaps this will be my new motto. "**Receive The Truth, Act on It, And See The Change.**"

Starting with one blow at a time. I recognized that I was in a war and my enemies wanted me destroyed. I fell off to sleep thinking that it was possible to fight back. While sleeping I saw this man appear unto me. His hair was black and he had a beard. His skin was olive color, not white or black. This man looked at me and said, "It's time to change." Suddenly, I felt a bolt of electricity hit my abdomen and I doubled up in bed. My mouth began to say "Thank you Jesus," over and over again. This thing scared me and I pulled the cover on my bed close around my neck.

The next morning I woke up and had a desire to pray for the first time. I went into the bathroom and knelt on the side of the bathtub and said. "Dear God, please make something of my life." Then I got up and got dressed. I didn't want anything to eat this morning. My appetite seemed to be totally gone.

I decided to go back to the mall. On my way to the bus stop I felt like I had just stepped off a spaceship. What happened to me? I kept trying to figure it out. The sky looked new! The grass looked new! I remembered the man in my dream and the power that hit my belly. It was real and it felt so good. Like a bolt of 220 electricity! I knew that I could not have stood that power any stronger. Josiephine, girl you are changed. I was somewhere that I have never been before. I still didn't know what happened to me. I walked around the mall and it seemed as if I was a million miles away. I couldn't focus on all those things that seemed to get my attention on yesterday. Suddenly I knew that I had to go back to the prayer meeting on Friday night.

9

Changed

Who would have thought, Josiephine De´Light is on her way to a prayer meeting? My new motto, "Receive The Truth, Act On It, And See The Change," was working for me! I had to receive the truth. Going to that prayer meeting changed my whole life, because of this very fact I am acting on this truth again. I am expecting to see change. This takes the struggle out of my life.

My hands look better today than yesterday simply because I saw that they were looking worn out. I got a manicure and brought some lotion. Now I see a change. Even the skin on my face looks better because I bought some face cream and each night and morning I moisturize my face and I do see a change. Not only in my face but somehow I feel better about myself.

I even lost two pounds this week. I finally received the truth about myself. I could keep on eating, not exercising and grow older and fatter which would and already had affected my health. I could end my life like that or fight with my new motto. I acted on the truth that I saw and made little changes that I could live with and I saw change. I liked the fact that I could see change.

I began to do a little more exercise and took potato chips out of my diet. As I continued to do this, change continued to occur. To people who saw me I might have looked the same but truth received was working on the inside and I knew it.

As I sat on the bus and traveled across town I wondered what was going to happen tonight. I still felt so different. The bus was pulling up to the church and I saw people coming from all directions going on the inside. No doubt whatever that power, presence and peace was falling in that building everybody wanted a piece of the action. Just to think it was free made me so happy. My budget couldn't have afforded it. Then who could I have gone to buy it from. How do you buy power, presence and peace? There was a definite presence that the peace and power flowed from. But, I have not seen the unseen hand.

As I opened the door to go in that peace embraced me. I felt tears of gratitude feel my eyes. I was so grateful that this thing was real. I so needed the peace to continue in my life. I was again greeted and told to help myself to the refreshments.

This time I was more observant of my surroundings. There was a red banner with fringes at the bottom and on the banner was written, "The Acts." The place looked like a restaurant. There were tables and chairs all over the place. A great sitting area up front that was real cozy. There were many interesting things around to see and plenty of purple and white flowers, lights galore all around. I saw the young teen who had read the bible the last time I was here, and I hoped that he would do so tonight.

All of a sudden this song came on, and I later found out that the Pastor wrote it.

"I'm Coming out of My Cocoon Today"

I'm going to spread my wings and fly away.
I'm coming out of these old wineskins to stay.
From now on I'll travel in a more
excellent way.
I'm free, free today.
I'll never go back to yesterday.
Let the world have their say.
From my purpose I'll never stray.
I was born to fly.
To the old things,
I've got to say goodbye.
There is someone beckoning for me
beyond the sky.
From now on I'll never have to sigh.
I hear the flutter of wings nearby.
I know that destiny draws nigh.

> *I must fly and aim high.*
> *I've got to release what's in me before I die.*
> *Greatness is calling for me.*
> *I smell sweet victory.*
> *I know I'll never retreat.*
> *I'll not receive the word defeat.*
> *Lord my faith looks up to thee.*
> *Oh Lamb of Calvary*

As I listened to each word it was as if these words were penned just for me. While the song was playing the pastor and another woman danced out in the open as if they were dancing for some royalty. What I thought were all black outfits, turned out to be glorious rays of sparkling colors as they demonstrated coming out of their cocoons.

From time to time they would bow to this unseen royal presence. The room filled with smoke right before my eyes. Tears of joy began to fall down my cheeks. There was power coming out of the garments they were wearing. By this time they were twirling all around the room and when they came over to me I experienced that sensation of electricity.

My hands flew up with all the other hands in the room. Even the little children's hands were up lifted. I was lost in this powerful presence. My hands were lifted straight up in the air as if by some unseen force! Next thing that I knew I was again saying "Thank You Jesus" over and over! My body began to move as if each part was trying to go in a separate direction! I felt wonderful and I never wanted this sensation or this presence to leave me!

Suddenly I thought this must be Jesus and then the most beautiful language began to come forth out of me like a river! Weights and burdens rolled off of me and new peace that passed all my understanding settled in me! That something that was missing from me all my life was in place now!

I received the truth. Afterwards, we gathered together to pray I acted on this thing. I couldn't help telling the people there that Jesus came into my life and I am changed!

10

Shocked

Here I am twenty-one days into my walk with the Lord and I get a bomb-shell dropped on my head. Jack calls and says, "That the house has been sold," just like that! Telling me that I had to be out in thirty days and that all he could give me was five thousand dollars! What was I to do? I had asked Jack for more and he said that he had over extended himself. Also that there were bills to take care of. I remember hanging up the phone in a daze. This I hadn't expected.

Things were going so much better since Jesus came into my world. I was a part of the church and faithfully attending bible classes. Vision on Thursday nights and Fragrance on Friday nights. I was learning so much. Also, it gave me new strength to deal with the things that were going on in my life. I was beginning to dream of a better day.

Suddenly I had to reach for my motto, "Receive The Truth, Act On It, And See The Change."

I found myself doing some soul searching. For years I had allowed my mind to become a wasteland! I planted nothing in it!

I allowed Jack to make all the family decisions, what to spend money on and what not to spend it on? It seemed to me in looking back that it was spent on him and not on me! I didn't even know how much money he made. I had no idea of what was in our savings accounts or checking accounts. Jack kept the checkbooks. I had blindly put all my trust in him. I was so eager to please him that I neglected myself.

I sent a message to myself saying, "It's all about Jack. Josiephine, you don't matter." I didn't have anyone that I could call and borrow twenty dollars from. I closed people out of my life. Jack was everything to me! I put all my trust in him. When he left, he left me bankrupt in every area of my life. I always gave him his way. Why didn't I stand up for myself? I don't believe I ever told Jack no. I allowed myself to be used and taken advantage of. Even allowing him to take my son away from me.

I could feel bitterness and anger beginning to rise up inside of me like a ragging sea! I started to think of ways that I could get revenge. Jack, had stolen from me and I wanted to get even! I wanted to tear him down like he tore me down! I was angry with Jack even though I allowed him the key to my world. I gave him free entry! This did not change the way I was feeling. I was so furious that I was shaking! I sat quietly for a moment and a still small voice spoke to me from down in my belly and said, "Will you allow bitterness, anger, unforgiveness, resentment and retaliation to steal your future."

The voice continued to speak. "Didn't you learn anything the first time around when you allowed Jack to steal from you? You were left bankrupt! Now you want to allow unforgiveness to bring in help and wreck your life! You can choose to live this day Josiephine, or you can get ready to die. For starters, the peace that has blessed your life will leave just as soon as you say yes to unforgiveness. Jo, it's your move!"

I felt my heart melt and I got down on my knees and asked the Lord to help me. Right then I said, "Lord I am giving you this unforgiveness, I can't afford it. The price is too high! Please show me the path that was laid out for me before I was born into this world? I realize that you saw this day coming and prepared a path for me to walk on." I could feel tears fall from my eyes. It felt like my insides were being cleansed out.

Sometime later I rose up with such a renewed peace. I felt a desire to think on my motto. "Receive The Truth, Act On It, And See The Change!" I, Josephine De´Light, do confess this day that, "I have been sleep for seventeen years with my eyes wide open." "It hurts but I have to move on."

I got up and called the Pastor and briefly informed her that my living arrangements had changed and to please inform me if she knew of a place that had a room or one bedroom apartment for rent. I told her that I couldn't afford to pay a lot. She said just that morning she noticed that there was a for rent sign for an apartment posted in front of one the storefronts up the street from the church. She described the location where the place was and I thanked her before hanging up the phone. I received the truth about myself and what was happening in my life, I acted quickly in calling to get information that I needed on the apartment.

Since I went to bible classes over in that area I might as well move to that area of town. It was as different as night and day compared to my beautiful neighborhood. But with my new found strength I knew I could do it. Change will be taking place as a result of my actions. Another truth was the fact that the classes on Vision and Fragrance were feeding me each time I went.

In those classes I heard things like, "There is a winner on the inside of me! The best is yet to come! God has a plan for my life! That I am unique! That I am an original! That there is no one like me!" I thought about all the flowers in the world and they all differed. Every snow flake is different! I don't have to be afraid to be unique! God made me this way. Those classes set me on fire and charged my battery. I felt a flicker of light go off in me that I could somehow make a living for myself.

I got up early the next morning and went over to check out that apartment. The outside of the building needed painting really bad. It was old and the hallways were very bleak looking. There were holes in the walls. Someone took the liberty to draw on the walls. The apartment was on the second floor. The door to the apartment looked sturdy enough. The apartment had a small kitchen, bathroom, small bedroom and surprisingly a larger size living room than I expected. There were three huge windows looking down on the street below. One of the windows had a broken pane.

This kind elderly lady looked anxiously at me to see if I approved of it. The price was a little more than I was prepared to pay but the heat was included in the rent so I said that I would take it. Mrs. Morgan, she and her husband were the property owners. They stayed in the other apartment across the hall from me. They had a storefront on the first floor that was rented out.

The walls in the apartment needed painting. I thought about how worried Mrs. Morgan looked and I realized that I wasn't the only one that had troubles. I made a point to try to give her an encouraging word when I saw her again.

When I got home I phoned Jack and told him to wire me the five thousand dollars. I told him that I had found an apartment. He sounded so surprise as if he thought that I would try to hang on to the house. As I hung up the phone I walked around the house and touched the furniture for the last time. Jack even had the nerve to sell most of the furniture with the house! The nerve of him! Some how this didn't rob me of my peace. I spoke to Lil' Jack on the phone and he sounded more friendly towards me. I decided that I would do some studying and afterwards I would do some packing. My motto was still helping me. "Receive The Truth, Act On it, And See The Change."

Receiving the truth for me was to always put the most important thing first in my life. When I was bankrupt an encounter with Jesus changed my life. I must always give him the choicest portions. Because of this I am changing and seeing things around me change

11

Starting over

Sitting and drinking coffee and checking the newspaper was proving unfruitful in my search for a job. However, I wasn't going to worry about it. He knows the path that I take. In a couple of hours I would be leaving this place that I spent years serving my husband in. I looked around the room and looked at the key that I would be leaving in the mailbox for the new owners.

I remembered the old rugged key to my new apartment and I wondered where it led. I would be walking through a new door in a matter of hours. I would be sleeping in a new place. This brought sadness to my heart. I had brought mattresses so at least I would have something to sleep on. I had boxed up some smaller items from the house that I felt entitled to take with me, Mixer, blender, microwave, toaster, etc., that I wanted.

I hired some movers that Mrs. Morgan knew that would move me at a good price.

I took one last glance at the house as the old moving truck was pulling away with me inside. I felt a pain hit my heart that I wasn't expecting. The memories came flooding back. I took a deep breath determined to face the future with one step at a time. Yes, I would take the necessary steps. I am coming out of my cocoon today!

I felt the wind from the open window blow on my cheek. I heard the birds singing and realized that no matter the neighborhood the bird always had a song to sing. I determined that I would do likewise. I would take a lesson that the birds were teaching and I would do likewise.

Could it be that this was where I lived? I stuck the key into the lock. Putting down my grocery bags on the table I looked around the room and saw it needed increase. Here was my motto rising up. I faced the truth. I was going to take action right now. I left out of the door just as quickly as I came in. I headed up the street to the hardware store to buy paint. I would paint every inch of these rooms. I chose a creamy white and lemon yellow. I made it back home, changed into work clothes and began to paint. Five days later I had the whole place painted.

I took my time and made sure I did my studies and went to classes at church. In class the power of God was so powerful, I jumped up and there was no music playing, I was jumping up and down shouting, "Thank you Lord," over and over again. I felt so free and so good. Others were shouting right along with me.

When I left the building I stopped to talk with one of the ladies attending the class, who had just started. She was so excited about the change that was taking place in her life also. After a few minutes we parted company.

The apartment was showing the increase. I brought some flowers to put on my cute little table I brought at a yard sale. The sisters hired me to work at L.A.P. & Freedom after they closed on the weekends. This kept me from having to touch my savings. I put three thousand dollars in a savings account and paid my rent up for a few months and if I am really careful I can survive until I get more work to do. I loved cleaning the hat shop. I still feel that peace in the shop. Now I know whom it comes from.

I smiled to myself because Mrs. Morgan came into my apartment and said it's beautiful and it feels so peaceful in here. I invited her to sit down and she quickly did so. Later, she rose to leave as if she really didn't want to go. I could see that you can get a blessing hanging around those Jesus people. One day I'm going to tell Mrs. Morgan the first time I experienced that peace and how she can get it in her apartment. But more than that, she needed it on the inside of her. I am so excited about going to heaven one day. But I got to live in this world until I get there!

Today I can say without a doubt that the only way to travel through this life is with peace, this can only come from Jesus. I love Jesus for he has made the difference in my life. I would not have made it without the Lord.

"Josiephine, look at you girl." I have lost forty pounds by continuing to apply my motto to my life. Each day I examine myself and receive the truth about what I see. Then make a motion to do something to counter act what I see. As a result I always witness a change.

I spend time with my Creator. Sometimes, I just sit quietly in his presence communing with him. Afterwards I am always refreshed and renewed. I drink living water and eat the bread of life each day from my Bible.

Surprisingly, Jack called one day to inform me about his plans for Lil' Jack. Afterwards he lingered on the phone asking me how I was doing? Which he didn't wait for an answer but followed it with another sentence. "Josiephine, I hope you're not still going to that church." I wanted to say, "what is it to you!" but I didn't. I said, "Jack, I certainly am and shall continue to do so."

Josiephine, you don't know anything about those people! "Jack it is not those people who turn me on. It is the one those people hang around!" "Don't tell me Josiephine, that you still believe in that Jesus stuff!" "No Jack, I am passed that. I have received that Jesus stuff and it works!"

"Josiephine, when Lil' Jack comes to see you don't you be trying to brain wash him." "Not only do I hope his brain is washed Jack, but I hope he gets washed all over!" "I'm warning you Josiephine!"

"Are you threatening me Jack? I have rights also and that is my son and I will not hide any good thing from him!"

12

Action

    This is a beautiful day. Lil' Jack is outside with the neighborhood kids playing. Now he seems to enjoy his visits. In the beginning when Jack started to drop him off for visits he stood outside starring at the place with his mouth open. After Jack drove off he reluctantly came inside with me. He seemed a bit more at peace after he came inside.

    I had taken what I had and put creativity with it and the results showed right away. But more that that, my home had the peace of a royal presence ready to saturate anyone that stepped into the room. Jesus had the room lit up.

    I wouldn't trade my old neighborhood where I came from for this apartment even though it was beautiful. There was no peace there. Jack and I seemed to get along well together but the two places are as different as night and day. I know that wherever I live in this life I have got to have this peace in my home.

    Lil' Jack ate his dinner with great relish. After eating he jumped up to go sit on the couch. Suddenly my motto came to my mind. "Receive the Truth, Act On It, And See The Change." What's going on here? I could feel the lift in my peace for a moment.

    This was a pattern that I had seen before trying to break loose in my house! Just as quickly as I felt my peace lift I told Lil' Jack to get his dishes off the table and put them in the sink. I couldn't have him growing up and getting married with this kind of pattern. I invested time in Lil' Jack's training him to perform in a way that would bring a blessing into his home. It's more blessed to give than to receive.

    Now after months and months invested in training Lil' Jack he knows what the pattern looks like. He knows to pick up after himself! It has even brought us closer. He told me this weekend that he showed the pattern to the housekeeper. When she saw his room that she actually smiled and said thank you. I started calling Lil' Jack, "Jack Jr." I wanted him to grow into his identity without a childhood name handicapping him in any way. It was time for me to weave a new thread into this pattern. Now he is outside playing with the neighborhood kids and there's much laughter coming from him as they played basketball.

Later on this evening I'll take him to L.A.P. & Freedom with me to help me clean. Yes, the truth has been instilled into him, "If a man don't work, he don't eat." Jack Jr. took to working with me as if it was in him all the while but he needed help releasing it.

I even started him a savings account at the neighborhood bank. Each weekend I take him to the bank with me. He deposits most of his earnings that I gave him for the work that he does with me on the job. Also, he is required to keep some out for an offering to the Lord when we go to class on Friday nights. Lil' Jack sees me make deposits into my own account even if it is only three dollars. The truth is that it will add up. Jack Jr., no longer hassles me about church. He says "I know it is in the pattern."

Lately I've been thinking about my sister's visit. What she spoke about our parents, asking for me to visit, was tugging on my heart. My peace was somehow being disturbed. Perhaps, it was time for me to pay them a visit. I decided then and there that I would go and get my bus ticket and make the fourteen-hour trip by bus.

Somehow the thought kept coming to me that I should fly. But this I pushed away. I'll not go into my savings to pay the price for a plane ticket. This thought kept pressing in on me and I would not do it. As it was I had put this trip off for a while. I had a sense that I should have gone some months ago but I wasn't ready.

Going on a bus would give me time to think of what to say. I decided to surprise my sister and not tell her that I was coming. I later learned that I couldn't be so stuck where my motto was concerned that I didn't allow for new prophetic truth to lead me in my decision making.

Sometimes you will have to readjust truth allowing space for weather bulletins. I learned a harsh lesson concerning this. "The Author who had given me "Receive The Truth, Act on It, And See The Change." He desired to be the breath behind the phrase.

13

Too Late

Here I am in my home-town where I grew up and everything looked so old and out dated and not at all big like I remembered. The population of this town when I grew up here was forty-thousand people. There were a lot of new buildings, and the old ones were torn down. Yet even with the new buildings the place looked small and kind of sad. The drugstore where I used to buy candy was gone and the building was empty. I could talk about a building standing but empty.

No dreams, no visions, no goals, no purpose, that's the way I ended up after being open for service to my husband all these years. Then one day I stood empty and drained just like this building and abandoned. Every time I see an empty building I want to remember the lesson that I learned. I could feel a trace of the pain that I experienced after being rejected by Jack.

At least my parents didn't walk out on me. In fact, I left them. All of a sudden I felt a leap in my heart. I really wanted to see my parents. Now that I think about it my parents were not really that bad. They worked hard and I never seem to have enough time with them. There were many times I can remember them saying, "Not now Josiephine, I'm tired." But they were never too tired to peep into my bedroom at night and say goodnight. Why am I having all these thoughts now? This place is stirring up some memories that I had forgotten.

There were those times that I needed to be taken to the dentist and my dad took off from work and took me and dad was really kind to me on those days. There was the time that mom sat up with me when I had the measles. Even my sisters and brothers were kind to me at those times. I saw a cab after walking around for a while and decided not to delay getting to my parents house.

As the cab pulled up to the house, after all these years it was still well kept. Looking at the flowers out front of the house caused me to think of the sisters for a moment. Why had I stayed away from my family all these years. Jack Jr. didn't even know his grandparents. In fact he had never seen them. I made a decision right then that my son would know his grandparents. Jack didn't have parents. Jack Jr. had only one set of grandparents and they were my parents. I wanted him to build some memories with them.

I thought about how at Christmas time the house was filled with search activities when I was a child. We always got plenty of surprises. There were decorations all over the place. In fact, at Christmas I remember my parents asleep in front of the fireplace. They both worked so very hard.

They wanted to make sure that I had a college education. I never took them up on their offer of college, because I left home right after I graduated from high school. Now I wondered why my sudden rush to get away.

My parents were always strict about my being home at a certain time. I felt if as though they didn't care about me. They made me do my homework and chores. Now that I think about it, wasn't that what a good parent should do? All these years I let slip by! Walking with Jesus has taught me a lot!

As I rang the door-bell I knew that I had to ask my parents to forgive me. I didn't even give them a phone call. I didn't send them a card on their anniversary. I didn't even allow them to see their grandson. If nothing else I should have been thankful because they gave me life. They were due respect simply because they were my parents. My heart lifted up at my new-found revelation, that my parents showed they cared for me. I couldn't wait to ask for their forgiveness.

The door suddenly opened and there stood my sister Marlo. She just starred at me with her mouth opened. I reached out and hugged her. My heart suddenly filled with love for her. She had moved in my parents home and took care of them. Here she stood before me a little thinner now, but with a peace on her face. She said, "Josiephine!" as if she was shocked to see me.

Then she asked me to come in. I saw how well kept the house was. There was furniture there that I didn't recognize. I kept looking around trying to see if mom or dad would come walking into the room. I had so much to say to them. I couldn't contain myself any longer. I asked where mom and dad were?

Marlo still gave me that strange look. Then she said, "Jo, they are gone." I looked at her and said gone where? I was preparing myself to sit down and wait for them. I sat on the couch and said that I wasn't in a rush and had come to stay for a few days. So I don't mind waiting. I asked Marlo what time did she think they would be back? Marlo took a deep breath and said "Josiephine they won't be coming back. Mom and dad died three months apart from each other."

I felt my world crumbling. In the background Marlo was saying that she had tried to get in touch with me. That I had moved and there was no forwarding address. No telephone where she could reach me."

It was as if I had disappeared. No this could not be happening to me! I wanted to ask my parents to forgive me. I wanted us to try and be a family again.

What was I to do with this yearning in my heart to see my parents? What was I to do with wanting to hear them call my name again? Suddenly I remembered daddy's smile. You mean I'll never see that smile again. What about the way mom would laugh? Would I ever hear that laugh again? You mean it's over just like that. I thought we were about to go on a journey as a new family. What was I to do with the embrace and kiss that I had for them? I felt tears rolling down my face. All the wasted days and wasted nights.

I'd come the long way around. My journey had been fruitless, I'd harvested little. I felt like I'd walked around and around in the wilderness. Why hadn't I seen the signs? I was too busy serving the wrong things. It had my full attention and I gave it my all.

I let it drain me with my approval every day. I gave it my applause. I locked myself in a place for years and didn't stick my head out to see what was going on in the world. I didn't give a thought to my parents. I was so busy serving what I thought was important. All the while I let life with my parents pass me by. Time wasted that I can never get back. If I could only turn back the hands of time.

I felt a scream rising up in my belly but nothing came out of my mouth. It stopped in my heart and just sat there. Now I know what real pain feels like. Jack hurt me! Took all that I gave him as his due. But Jack could be replaced with someone else who could really love me. But the time lost with my parents could never be replaced. All the golden moments lost. I didn't invest anything. There is a place in my heart that is empty. Can it ever be filled?

That night I couldn't sleep. I kept tossing and turning thinking that I would wake up from this nightmare. I woke about one in the morning. I went over to the desk and sat down in the chair and began to write.

"Why so much pain?
There are tears falling
from my eyes like rain.
I have only myself to blame.
Now I know that life is not a game.
From this experience what shall I gain?
I don't think I'll ever be the same.
There are some storms that you can't tame.
I'm in a valley so low
that I wanna change my name.
I don't want notoriety and I don't want fame.
I got no joy and no song to sang.
I wish I could start all over again.
I hear a small voice in my ear.
Saying, hold on my child I am near.
I'll wipe away your every tear.
Do not worry and please don't fear.
For you I'll make this a very good year.
I am the potter and you are the clay.
I am working on you day by day.

Walk this way. There is no time to play.
I'm raising you up for a brand new day.
Continue on and do what I say.
You can count on me,
I'll lead you all the way.
Never forget that I got a plan for you.
There is something for me that you must do.
Rejoice for I have already
mapped out the way through!
HELL IT SELF CANNOT HOLD YOU!
There is none that can stop what I do.
Get ready for I'm going
to reveal myself to you!
Then you will know!
By my show!
That I rule below!
I AM
UNSTOPPABLE! UNBEATABLE! UNSEARCHABLE!
UNMOVEABLE! UNTEACHABLE! UNREACHABLE!"

14

The Transformation

I've been home now for a week and I haven't been out of this apartment. Life seem to have lost it's glow. Only a few weeks ago I had hope for the future. Now I feel all dried up. I've not prayed and have not been to Bible class. It is like I've run out of gas. I've got to get out of this slump.

This place is not the place for me. There is no joy here and my peace is gone. Lord what is wrong with me? Old habits want to come back on me. I had chips in the house when Jack Jr. would visit and I found myself sitting and eating all of those chips. What's wrong with me? What a difference a few days can make. Within days of my trip home my mom died before I could get there.

Looking back and as I think about it I could have gotten there. But I refused to pay the fare. I was stuck on saving for a rainy day. Not knowing that it was raining at the moment of my decision to take the bus and not fly.

Will I ever be able to forgive my self for this? I took quite a risk and lost. I'll never see my mom again. At my parents grave sight before I left I tried to speak to them and there was no real comfort for me being there.

My future looks so bleak. I can't seem to get a good night's sleep. Lord where do I go from here? I hadn't prayed in days. "Josiephine you have got to get a whole of yourself." I hadn't told anyone that I was back in town.

Have I traveled this long way to get stuck here? I caught a glimpses of my self in the mirror. My appearance was so much better. I had lost a considerable amount of weight. However I was still over weight. My hands looked so much better.

At that moment I reached over to get my hand cream. I kept hand cream near so I could lotion my hands when I needed too.

Then all of a sudden it seemed my motto came up from my belly. "Receive The Truth, Act On It, And See The Change."

Right then memories came flooding back. I remembered when I was so low I couldn't seem to go any lower then God stepped into my life. Oh how I needed a dose of the truth. I was hurting and feeling abandoned. Right then I got down on my knees and just put my head down. I didn't say anything I just stayed in that position. I was stuck in a hard place. I cried out softly, "Lord help Me, Lord you are my peace. Please forgive me for turning away from you when I needed you most." It was right then that I heard that still voice again saying.

"It is time to build.
Each day daughter
you must plant something new.
Then you can see the results of something new.
You have always got to plant to see change
Come forth in a different dimension.
I'll walk you through.
You cannot afford to get stuck.
You must continue to build.
Here you are sitting in this apartment for days.
Repeating the old ways and habits.
Don't you know that those things
will take you over?
Do you want to go back in chains today?
You are allowing yourself to be bound.
Life is not a game.
You are not to be up and down.
You got to go pass your feelings!
Feelings will make you dysfunctional.
They will cripple you.
You got to move out Josiephine.
You cannot afford to linger
Into the valley of do nothing.
Destiny is calling for you to come forth!

You'll build your destiny.
You'll flow into destiny.
Move on out and don't be afraid.
Surely I will be with you. "

    The apartment was so quiet and I knew that the atmosphere had changed. The peace was back in the air. The royal presence was standing up again. I felt so light. How long did I rest in the Lord's presence? It was dark outside now and I felt as if a bright light was shining. I couldn't wait to get to class on this week.

    Suddenly I knew just what I wanted to do with my life. I wanted to start a restaurant. Not just any kind of restaurant. But I wanted the kind of place that gave you Peace to eat. I wanted a place where they could experience joy. I wanted music flowing through the atmosphere.

    The color scheme must be something special. I wanted a place that would be used to touch a life. If it had not been for the hat store, I might not be here today. That store carried a royal presence. I shall never forget the peace that I experienced every time I went there. Even on bad days I would always feel better after I left.

    I could remember how that peace in the air was alive and would reach out and touch me. Later, I found out the real deal. These sisters spent time with Jesus and because they did He spent time with them.

    This one thing for sure as I go forth and if I hope to achieve my dream I must spend time in his presence. Oh, I must make my plans! In our class we were taught that without a vision people perish. I don't have to be a hopeless case now. I got a vision. It brings joy to my heart! I know it's the Lord! He's leading me. He has a wonderful plan for my life!

    The next day I went out and brought some materials and paint samples. I didn't have the money to start a restaurant but I had a great big dream, which was the needed ingredient. You can have a lot of money and no vision, then what will it profit you? Even though I needed seed money for my plan, my dream was good enough for a starter.

I put those samples on pieces of cardboard and played with the colors. Pretty soon I had my color scheme. I was so excited. I would use lemon yellow, creamy white, purple and turquoise for my basic color scheme. Then I would throw in a splash of other colors here and there. I could feel new life surge through me. I had to put my project down because it was time for my classes at church.

Who would have ever thought that I would ever be rushing off to church and loving it? This class was dealing with real life issues. It was stirring me to reach for my dream. I was doing just that. I remember what the Lord had told me. Build into your destiny. I made a promise that I would do just that.

I had put away some money. Even Jack had given me some money a few weeks ago. He must have felt guilty. He knew that I was having it hard and he had cheated me. I was determined not to ask him for anything and I didn't. I don't know whether Jack Jr. told him to share the loot. Ha ha, listen at you girl. However, God did it! I took that money and put it right into my account. After I paid my tithes and offerings.

I even gave Jack Jr. a few dollars of it. Four thousand dollars looked real good added onto what I already had. I would pray and ask the Lord just how to do this thing. I would go straight to the top. His door is always open to me. He speaks my language ha ha.

15

Vision

After getting up this morning I thought how I shared with Jack Jr. about my plans for the restaurant. I hadn't expected him to get so excited. I knew families would be eating there and so it pays to have a younger influence involved.

I was so blessed because he suggested something that blew me away. He suggested fish aquariums in the restaurant in different spots. You should have seen us. We had books out on the floor as we looked through one book after another. We put together how we wanted our fish aquariums to look.

We picked white rocks so that the color of the fish would show and we decided on saltwater tanks. The fish are more vivid in colors. We wanted to have the same color fish in the different tanks. We would try to get purple, turquoise, lemon yellow and creamy white fish. With the white fish, which we hope to find with little markings of purple, turquoise and yellow, we will put down purple gravel. That pleased us so that we decided to just do turquoise gravel with the yellow fish. This is so exciting. We were building! The amazing thing is, as we built our dream on the cardboard posters, in our hearts the hope began to build.

Tomorrow we decided to go to the fish stores and see the price for this project and find out about the upkeep. Jack Jr. was so happy with this dream that we were building on. I made a mental note that, when I finished my plans for the restaurant that one day I would build my dream house and decorate it on cardboard squares. But for now there was so much more to do. When Jack Jr. left he made Jack promise to bring him back a day earlier so that we could continue to build.

We needed to spend time on how many rooms we needed and what we were to use each for.

The kitchen area had to be considered. In the main dining area we had decided on the color of the table and chairs. Oh this was such a blessing. Everyday I kept planting. I would look in books to see what kind of dishes that I wanted to use, the type of silverware that I wanted, tablecloths, napkins, floral arrangements on the tables had to be considered. What kind of pictures that I wanted to put on the walls if any. What types of uniforms the help would wear. The floor covering had to be considered. What area of town did I want to do this venture in?

Jack Jr. came back a day earlier and had a stack of magazines with him. I was so pleased. We decided go to downtown and eat. We chose a restaurant that was not so expensive but would allow us to build while we were there. We took the restaurant apart examining the decor, the servers, the dishes, silverware, the glasses, tablecloths and napkins, walls, etc. We even checked out the restrooms. Jack Jr. took the men's and I took the women's. As our food was being prepared we timed how long it took. We compared notes at the table. It was so exciting. I did not expect the preparation of this dream to be so life giving. My son and I were coming together in a greater way just by our sharing this project. The food was excellent and we left a tip as we were leaving. The server was good at what he did, and this made our dinner experience a happy one. The atmosphere in the restaurant was filled with music but missing that life giving touch.

As we were leaving the restaurant it began to rain. This made us think that we needed a certain type of lighting for all kinds of weather. The Lord was not missing a beat. He was leading me through this building process.

The sisters were so excited about what we were working on. You would have thought they were the ones starting the restaurant. I thrived off the encouragement. Although there were those that I shared with that tried to put my fire out. Always at night I would get with the Lord and ask him what was the next thing that we needed to work on. I would ask the Lord if what I had put together so far met with his approval.

There were things like cleaning supplies to price. We needed to check out the kinds of charges that the gas and electric would cost. Zoning availability for the building. I was sleeping so good at night. I rose up each morning with a goal to tackle for that day.

I was running with my vision and then got a bit of bad news. My job cut some of my hours. But the dream was on fire and even this bad news couldn't quench it. I decided to work on the menu and what I thought it should look like and what I wanted to serve. I decided on things like fried chicken, fish, meatloaf, steak, roast beef, turkey and dressing. Also, the basic mash potatoes, macaroni and cheese, baked potatoes, some vegetables and I even threw in some burgers and fries, also all kinds of pies. I was skilled in cooking a large variety of foods. But I was choosing those things I thought family people liked the best. I'll have plenty of soft drinks. Also ice cream. I would do some of the most popular dinners that are around.

That night as I prepared to talk with the Lord I could tell that something was up. My peace was lifting. I asked the Lord what was wrong. The Lord told me "Throw out the food list that I had prepared to serve." He said "Why half step. Why not go first class all the way. Above all else that I needed to be concerned about the food I'll serve."

16

The Messenger of Love

This morning I got up thinking how my spirit ate and loved the taste of good things. My soul was always blessed from these experiences. I remembered the experience of going to the sister's shop and experiencing all that peace. It was not a surface peace, you could eat it. It touched my life. I remembered the colors in the decor, it was a treat to me somehow because there was a taste in those colors. They seemed to have a divine touch. They stirred me.

There must be things with the breath of God upon them. These things picked my spirit up in such a way that it has not departed from me. The food that I serve must have this same impartation upon it. I want people to have a life changing experience as they eat in my restaurant. If Adam and Eve could eat something that was forbidden and it robbed them of the good life. Then, surely I could serve food that flowed in the will of God that would bring a blessing to my customers.

First, I would focus on those things that grew out of the ground and give them a bit more thought. What was the Lord getting at. Secondly, I thought about the apple, a beautiful piece of fruit, The smell of an orange or lemon. Quite heavenly. The pineapple or a bunch of grapes. The watermelon, peaches, pomongrantes how unique they are.

For so many years I took these gifts from God for granted. I just ate it not even thinking about the Author of the fruit. Not thinking about the message that was behind the fruit. The message said "I love you Josiephine De´Light." I had you in mind when I created this fruit. I just didn't throw something together for you but my heart went into it. I put love all in the fruit. The taste, the smell, the touch, the color, and the education.

The fruit was able to reproduce. Surely if he made the fruit to reproduce then he wanted reproduction in my life. God must have put that same ability within me to reproduce. "Josiephine girl, there are seeds of greatness within you." Suddenly I knew that my restaurant was inside of me and it was being birthed.

I knew right then that I had to do unusual things with this fruit in my restaurant that people could eat it but not just physically but spiritually also. I wanted this fruit to speak to them. This lead me to build a special station in the restaurant that people could go to and serve themselves. I called it, "The Place of De´Light."

In doing this section Jack Jr. came over and we cutout all the fruits, vegetables, and nuts that we could find. Then, we focused on our display station. We decided to build this food section in a huge mountain.

First, we would have beds of green lettuce, with all kinds of fruit to make the most unusual salads. Then we decided to circle this whole section with pineapples around it. It would allow for twelve people at a time to serve themselves, as we grew we would enlarge this section.

Secondly, we would put sweet onions around the next level building it up with mounds of raisins, and strawberries in a circle. There would be circles of peaches, and all kinds of nuts and fresh garden tomatoes. We would slice the cucumbers in extraordinary ways and circle them around the mountain.

Thirdly, we would have mounds of grapes of all different colors, and the bananas' would be left in their peeling for color and the beauty of them. The bananas' could be sliced on the salads at their table.

Last, on the mountain we would put all kinds of peppers, melons, squash, blueberries, and so much more. We would have to have a platform especially built for this setup, but it could be done.

Then, we would have fresh dressings with my special recipes. There is one dressing I am so fond of that I dump fresh crushed pineapples in to make that's heavenly. The calories would be of such that a person could help himself or herself and not worry.

To make this a really fun project, we decided to do my fresh baked turkey recipe with my special seasoning spices on them. We'd have whole turkeys on display and on special stands next to "The Place of De´Light Garden." They would be kept moist and warm at all times.

Also for those who don't care for turkey we would do my baked chicken recipe with my special seasoning spices on them. Jack and Jack Jr. always loved it when I would prepare these dishes.

Now it is time to take these dishes and make a living from them.

However the more I think about this adventure, it is more than making a living that's going on here. There seem to be such a flow and enjoyment as well. This is something that I always loved and wanted to do, and I am very good at it.

I've always loved learning new recipes because I wanted to please Jack. Now, I want to please the Lord and Josiephine. I want to make a contribution to the life of another. I wasn't gifted to do what the sisters have done, but I could use what was inside of me and let it flow out to humanity.

Life was full of struggles at times, and so when people pull away for a meal outside of their homes I wanted not just their money, but I want them to have an experience with this royal presence that had flooded my life.

When families come in I want them to consider the wonders of creation. Hopefully with all those fish aquariums this would be a great spark in that direction. I want to flow in my destiny so that the God I serve could be seen and experienced at all times.

17

The Next Level

Sitting at my cute little table, drinking coffee, I was enjoying the sun streaming through the window. As I looked around the apartment I was so pleased. It showed what could be done with creativity.

The place was not what I was accustomed to, however, Mrs. Morgan loves to come in and sit down for coffee when she comes for the rent. She says it is so beautiful in here. I offered to help her bring new life into her apartment. She jumped at the opportunity. We have been working on her apartment little by little and the change is dramatic. Who would have ever thought that just a floral arrangement on the table could make such a difference in her place.

I was brought back to my present surroundings by a knock at the door. This was my day off and Jack was dropping Jack Jr. off. So I rushed to open the door and there stood Jack. This really surprised me. I invited him in while Jack Jr. stayed outside with his friends that live in the neighborhood.

I braced myself for whatever Jack was about to say. He never really has any encouraging words to say to me. Today, he didn't seem his old sure self. He asked me, "how was I doing?" He even said, "I see you've lost a lot of weight." Not that I looked nice or anything like that. Then he said, "He was sorry about how everything worked out, but it was for the best."

Jack then began to ask me about what was going on with my life. This surprised me. He never in all the years that I've known him has he asked me what was going on in my life. I told him about the building project that was going on. I was building on my future. Jack said that, "Jack Jr. was a changed young man. That our son was so much happier and that he was glad about

18

It Came To Pass

As I stood surveying the place, I saw those things we had built on paper manifested before my very eyes. Even though it is not on the scale that it would one day be. I was finally through all the inspections, permits, licenses and other tedious matters.

We could move forth with the decor. We had the fixtures in place, the ovens, sinks and the special restaurant equipment that we could get at this hour, and a large freezer and refrigerator that was quite large. We were well pleased with the project.

The flooring was down. And this cost a bit more than I planned on, but the color fit well with the color scheme that we planned. The tile was charcoal gray with purple and turquoise spots in it.

We got small tables and chairs, to accommodate the sides of the place. The tables and chairs are made of blond wood. They were not new but were in good condition and all matched. The color flowed wonderfully with the color scheme. We put small vases of creamy white flowers with sprigs of turquoise and purple.

Jack gave Jack Jr. his charge card and said to please let him treat us to the fish aquariums. I graciously received the offer. We purchased four tanks. Thanks to the men at the church we had the platform for the fish tanks built. The walls had been torn out in four spots and the aquariums would be enclosed in the walls. The tanks were close to fifty gallons in size.

The affects were breath taking. The lighting in the tanks showed the beauty of the fish. The white fish with purple stripes were on the lemon yellow gravel with hints of purple in the tank. There were turquoise fish on white gravel with hints of purple in the tank. The purple fish had hits of yellow on them and they had turquoise gravel and plenty of large white rocks.

The last tank had lemon yellow fish on purple gravel with a lot of white stones also.

The most exciting thing about this place was how that royal peace settled on everything as if to say I am well please with this place. When people entered the door they talked about the peace and the beauty of the place. Some came for coffee even before we were opened just to sit in the atmosphere. I knew then that we were on the right track.

Jack Jr. was taking to the business like a fish in water. He was very detailed in keeping up with the money and the bills. Carefully he would make room for all our files. He picked this up going on business trips and hanging around his dad. Who would have thought that through the pain of being separated from my son that God would send me back a blessing with gain?

Next we set up our sound system and of course I got nature sounds with music. All different kinds of sound. I loved the waterfall sounds the best with harp music in the background.

Near the rear of the restaurant we displayed "The Place of De´Light." It was on a smaller scale but it had all the beautiful vegetables, fruits, nuts and off to the side of it the baked turkeys and chicken. As each customer served themselves at "The Place of De´Light" they would have the beauty of the special lighting, the splendor of the fish aquarium, along with the special affects of the music, serving as a backdrop into this peace that they would be experiencing. We made sure our bathrooms were decorated in the same color tones. They flowed right along with everything else.

We passed out flyers, and we got some astounding business through word of mouth customers. Factory workers came on the weekday and went back and got their families on the weekends and brought them to the restaurant.

When you stepped into the restaurant it was like stepping into another world. The peace on the inside embraced you. Most people lingered, and this made people have to stand in line on the outside, but they didn't seem to mind. They said it was well worth it just to sit back and relax. They enjoyed the benefits of the atmosphere as well as the food. Many loved "The Place of De´Light" stand. We kept it replenished. Mrs. Morgan worked with me and one of her duties was to keep the bar replenished with the needed items.

We always kept plenty of the fresh baked turkeys and chickens. There were other dishes that were popular. Beds of fresh stings beans filled with tomatoes, onions, garlic, basil with slices of turkey, topped off with fresh cheese, served with fresh homemade dinner rolls.

Of course by now I had to quit my job. But I loved coming to work and getting here early in the morning. I would just enjoy the peace. I had filled large bottles of olive oil with frankincense and stones to match the decor in the room and put them in various locations in the restaurant. I loved the beautiful paintings we picked out. Pictures of the sunshine on fresh green trees. Some with a few cottages and flowerings the same color tones.

One of the house specials was baked apples and sweet potatoes topped with pecans served on flat cornbread with a little fresh cream. Sweetened with honey. A somewhat unusual treat. Sometimes we would top it off with raisin.

Each day we would have special items cooked. We continually changed certain items so that the customers could experience a variety. I want them to experience the great God of variety. When I would cook all those meals for Jack and new desserts daily, I never thought that I would now be doing that very thing to make a living. We were doing excellent. We were making our salaries and paying all the bills on time.

19

The Same Pattern

Sitting here enjoying a cup of freshly squeezed orange juice I'm looking at the restaurant and enjoying the cleanliness of the place. I remember the first time I walked into L.A.P. & Freedom the place was so clean and alive with peace. Who would have thought that I would end up using the same color scheme that they used at the store in my restaurant? I smiled as I remembered how excited the sisters were about the restaurant. Of course, they are some of our greatest customers. They bring people here and pay for their food so they can share this experience with them.

What a wonderful thing to share what you have with others! I am so glad that Jesus shared His peace with me. I value it to this day and know that I cannot survive without it, That's why I have special rates for the elderly, and sometimes I have a day for the aged as I call them. When families bring them, the aged people get their food on the house.

Jesus gave me something valuable that changed my life and I want to give out something valuable that would change the life of another. Already we are planning an expansion. We've been looking around at property that we can purchase for opening another restaurant. Of course we would call it Josiephine De´Light. "Come On In & We Will Treat You Right," is one of our favorite sayings. To treat a person right is to treat one the way you desire to be treated. I know what it is to be taken for granted. To serve and never be appreciated for it. I want my customers to know that before they walked into the door I was thinking about them, their comfort, peace, rest, and even their future.

You never know where a person is. They could come in with the intent of ending their lives. Just by coming here and seeing that someone cared enough to reach out to their spirit, could be the thing to change them and to let them know that this place was used to bring them back to their senses, because it offered peace. Love is in the air, and what they could see physically was reaching out to touch them. Also what they couldn't see was reaching out to touch them.

My dream was growing and I needed my income to grow with it. Jack Jr. and I continued to make our trips to the bank putting our money away. I stayed with the motto that worked for me. "Receive the Truth, Act On It & See the Change," brought such a change in my life. To this day I still keep hand lotion near to keep my hands moisturized.

You stay with the same pattern that works for you. Why would you discard something that has brought a change and momentum into your life? I can wrap it up in one word, "Jesus." I don't know a lot about the different religions, but I do know about a relationship that has changed my life outside the walls of a building.

I was so surprised when Jack came by one night. Jack Jr. is driving now, so I wondered why he would come pass. He came in the door and was dressed to kill. He sat down at a table, and I went over to greet him and to see whatever did he want. He said he was going out to eat and thought about this place and that he knew that the best cook in town was here, and he wanted only "The Place of De´Light." I told him it was self serve. He smiled, saying, "He didn't mind." I watched him as he went to serve himself thinking to myself, what a switch, Jack getting his own food. I never thought I would see that day.

He came back to the table with piles of pineapples, sliced sweet onions, green peppers, on a bed of lettuce, his plate was loaded with tomatoes, raisins, peaches, carrots, broccoli, grapes, spinach leaves with piles of sliced fresh baked turkey and chicken on the side. We use oversize plates at "The Place of De´Light," so our customers could De´Light themselves. Jack certainly did and fixed his plate with such an artistic style. I was impressed. He then went to the fresh bread section and chose four different types of yeast rolls. I use to make them for him.

He sat down and ate with such a relish and didn't seem to mind being at the table by himself. A few minutes later Jack Jr. came in and was so pleased to see his dad. He pulled up a chair and sat down and talked with him. This brought back memories of how things use to be. I am so glad that those things no longer had a sting for me. I had forgiven and moved on.

The truth is, that I discovered that it does not profit to take yesterday's pain into your tomorrow. It was a process but it paid off. Every painful experience represented so much weight. Even on our bodies, excess weight will hinder us in many areas. So will weight that you cannot see with the physical eye. You may not even be aware that you are carrying this excess weight. But I learned to measure it by the peace I carry.

When I am full of peace it can flow out to others. When my peace is not where it should be, I am the first to know it because I am accustomed to having peace. Peace and I are not strangers. When my peace is not where it should be, I get together with the Lord. I know immediately that something is out of order. So I had to release a lot of hurts and pain over the years.

20

Morning Prayer

The workers and I had grown accustom to gathering together before God to ask him to please bless our day before the restaurant opened. We would ask him to bless each customer that came in and to help us to make this an enjoyable experience to each person that came in to eat on that day.

Afterwards we would each set out to do our different duties. Mrs. Morgan would set up "The Place of De´Light" with all the veggies, fruits and nuts. Then she would set out the seasoned baked turkeys and chicken. Sarah dealt with the entire section of homemade breads and yeast rolls.

It took a while to get the extra help we needed. First, we needed to get to a place where we could pay salaries. Then, we needed someone who loved the atmosphere and enjoyed the work. I taught Sarah the things that were in me as I saw that she was dedicated to the task. When Sarah and I sat down for lunch she and I would talk and share. I loved hearing her input.

She shared with me the other day how working in this environment fed her spirit. It added to who she was. She was already gifted to do the work. Now she felt like she was at home. She said there was a fulfillment on the inside of her. I am sure that she could have made more at a larger establishment, however, she chose to work along side of us.

As we grew we made sure that the salaries of our employees grew also. Every other month we got together with the workers for a meeting to see where we were headed in the future. One young man was saving for college. We all encouraged him on. Some wanted to grow with the restaurant. One day they hoped to train others to do what they are doing, so they could fill another position that called for their expertise as we grew.

Sarah and I took the vision classes at church so we always had a lot to talk about. We continued to encourage each other to go for our dreams, to aim high. She was always on time for work.

The customers sent her words of encouragement after tasting the breads that she freshly baked each day. This freed me from having to bake and I could do other needed things. Sarah kept the bread in the server stand fresh, warm and buttered at all times. We kept the bread stand and the baked turkeys and chickens with our special seasonings near "The Place of De´Light."

The word continued to spread concerning the restaurant. We had people calling in wanting to make reservations for parties of twenty-five to a hundred people so that they could come and eat together. Sometimes we would have to book special dates for them.

On one of these special events I twisted my ankle. This hindered me from being able to flow from table to table to greet our guest. We like the feel of calling our customers, guest.

It was almost time for the guest to arrive and Jack Jr. came into the kitchen with a big smile on his face. He said that he had solved our problem. He called Jack to come in and greet our customers for us and make them feel welcome. I thought to myself, "Yes he would be good at that."

Ten minutes later Jack came through the door. He looked a little uneasy. He greeted me politely and said that he was glad to help out. Jack Jr. quickly filled him in on what he would be doing. He told his dad that he was to see to everyone's comfort and answer questions about the restaurant.

People would often ask where did the idea come from to set the restaurant up like we did. They wanted to know about the different recipes we used, and all sort of questions. Even about the waterfall music and where the idea came from.

They loved the feel of the place. They would comment on how peaceful it was. Of course they love the fish all around and even the color scheme. I found out later that Jack was more informed than I knew. Jack Jr. had been a constant source of information. Always sharing with him about what we were into and our dreams and vision for the future.

21

Peace is Contagious

I found out later that Jack Jr. had been sharing with his father Jack the importance of the right atmosphere, and the main ingredient had to be peace. Jack Jr. had been walking in his relationship with the Lord a few years now. I never shall forget what Jack Jr. said to me the night he asked the Lord Jesus to come into his life.

He said, "Mom I live with dad in a big beautiful house, with plenty room, and we have all the modern appliances, but when I'm away from your place I don't feel that quietness in the air. When I'm at your place mom, there is something that wraps around me, and I love the feel of it. It is peace, but it is alive! I know that even Mrs. Morgan loves to hang out in your apartment.

When we go to L.A.P. & Freedom I love that peace that I feel in the air. When we go to worship with the sisters, that peace, just builds and build until I feel so warm on the inside. Mom, dad and I need this peace. I want to meet Jesus." on that night Jack Jr. received the Lord Jesus Christ.

Several days later he came over and said that there was a change in the atmosphere in their house. Even my friends say that our home feels different. Jack Jr. led all his friends to Christ. How exciting!

The other day something else wonderful happened. Mrs. Morgan allowed me to introduce her to Jesus. Every time I see her now she has a smile from ear to ear. She said that the atmosphere in her home has changed and that there is peace all in the air.

I know Jesus is saying, "It is time to start building again." Jack Jr. and I began to lay out the plans for the new restaurant. We didn't have the money in our hands as of yet. But, we have a big dream. With the private parties coming as often as they were, one day we would be in position to go to the next level. The money was pouring in and we made sure that we always saved a portion. It was great to see how Jack pitched in to help from time to time.

One night after all the guest were gone, Jack Jr. was doing the receipts for the day and Jack Sr. came into the kitchen after saying good night to the last customer. He sat down and Sarah brought him a cup of coffee and some bread and Jack looked at me and said that he had no idea what it took to cook and serve like I did.

"Josiephine, for years you had this gift locked up on the inside of you and I was a partaker of this gift. Please forgive me for taking your gift so casually as if it my due. I really took you and your gift for granted. I had no idea the work you put forth to make my coming home to eat a pleasant experience. I took you so carelessly."

"When I wanted my friends over for dinner. Like the day you told me the weather was going to be to bad for a cookout, I just told you to prepare for them. I brought a slicker and a new state-of-the-art gas grill thinking that would suffice my ego. I didn't ask if you felt like it or not. I knew you had it in you to make dinner happen at any time. I didn't consider that you might have wanted to rest, or that you may have wanted to just chill. I used that gift of serving that you have to feed my ego. Please forgive me Josiephine, I've watched how hard you all work around this place. Like a few months ago when you twisted your ankle. I got a good look at some things that I never saw."

I told Jack that I had forgiven him a long time ago. And that's the reason that I am where I am today. I traveled light and didn't bring bags of dead weight into my future. "It took the Lord to help me. Believe me there were times that I've had some hard struggles Jack. Like the time when you walked off and took my son. That was the day that broke my heart. In looking back, I thought it was a very bad day. But, there was someone who was thinking about Josiephine. Jack you meant it for evil and your selfish reasons but God meant it for my good. Because of what happened I saw, and I am seeing now, and shall continue to see a brighter day. I have learned that through pain there can be great gain."

"When I thought you had hit me with your hardest punch you threw another and stole the love that my son should've had for me. However, at that time I was just a servant for Lil' Jack as I was yours. If things had continued as they were I would have not have had a true relationship with Lil' Jack. Now Jack Jr. and I talk. And I am not afraid to tell him anything. I have now had the opportunity to teach him some valuable lessons that will be with him when I'm dead and gone. When I step to the other side my son will not be left empty or shallow."

"Sometimes when he did not want what I had to give him I spoon-fed him. Then I gave him a bottle, now he drinks out of a glass. I had to invest quality teaching in our son. It took time, starting with the dishes being taken off the table after he had eaten and put into the sink. It took me telling him to pick up his own clothes off the floor in the bathroom and clean the tub after he got out of it."

"Making sure he gave tithes and offerings to the Lord. Also he learned the necessity of saving money back for his future. He learned that it was a blessing to open the door for the elderly. He learned that love is not allowing him to have his way all the time. God gave me the opportunity to speak into my son's life things that will be with him as an adult and again, even when I'm gone. We talk all the time and he won't have to wonder what I think about this or that. I tell him now!"

22

Smashed to Recovery

Jack Jr. came through the door and wanted to know if we could go tomorrow and look at buildings. I said, "Sure, why not." One thing I knew was that we had a great big dream to own a chain of restaurants and a great big God that was able. Jack Jr. thanked his dad for helping out and went back to finish his work in the office. Jack continued to sit and drink coffee. "I told him after I suffered the second blow. You came back and kicked me in the belly."

"You sold the house without telling me, and you gave me a few dollars and then Jack you put your foot down and smashed me in the ground when you sold all the furniture with the house and never once asked my thoughts. I thought you cared for me as a person if nothing else. But your kind of love I am afraid of. But when you kicked me out Jesus took me in."

"I'm building with my experience in mind. I want to help those along the way who may have to travel the same street that I've had to travel on. I want to be able to feed the hungry. I know what it is to be hungry. Hungry for food and hungry for the love of a husband and child that said that I had no value."

"I know what it is to have no clothes, no love to cover me, no peace to cover me. I know what it is to be a prisoner. Locked in outside prison bars. Locked in someone else's opinion of who they think I am. I want to build a home one day for the homeless. I want to share with them that Jesus has a plan for their lives. I want to teach them that they can have a big dream and that it is possible to see it come to pass. I want to teach them about building for the future. It starts in the mind and the heart."

"I remember when you would come into the neighborhood driving your big fancy car and drop Jack Jr. off. You looked so tall and handsome, but I thought how looking at the outside cover can get you in a whole lot of trouble. Hot on the outside but your insides were so cold. I'd only have a dime in my pocket and I never said a word to you. Jesus taught me how to build for the future. I saw a better day. I wonder sometimes how you could have treated me that way. I know that I allowed you to, but you participated in a way that left me bankrupt. This was my wake up call and for that reason I am glad that it happened as I look back on it."

"Now because of the pain I am where I need to be. I don't know what all the future holds for me, but there is a seat in my heart that only Jesus can sit on. No man will ever sit there again and it is impossible to fill his seat. This I do know. Perhaps one day I may even marry. But I will be a free woman in that marriage. Not a man's prisoner nor a prisoner in my mind."

Jack suddenly stood up and said, "As you were speaking I was listening and a thought came back of something that happened a long time ago."

"When I was a youth I was outside playing with a friend of mine, my friend had a young puppy. As we were all playing around outside I stepped on the pup's paw. The pup let out such a painful scream that I can hear it until this day. I reached down to make sure he was going to be okay. I was so sorry that I hurt that puppy. A little later I was taken to another foster home. But as I stand here it has hit me to some degree how I have hurt you and didn't give you the care that I showed that puppy on that day. Can you ever forgive me? I can't change the past Josiephine but I can change what I do in the future. Do you think that you can let the past go?"

As I sat and listened to Jack I wondered how we even got to this conversation. I told Jack that I had already forgiven him. I did it to please Jesus. I was hurt so very bad but Jesus taught me how to forgive by faith and not to be blocked by my feelings. Then the Lord removed the taste of bitterness from my heart."

"Jack put yourself in my place. What if I had taken advantage and hurt you as you hurt me? Weigh each act. What if I used you like you used me? Like a dog going out to relieve itself. At least the dog will sometime try to cover up where he has relieved itself outside. But you never looked back to see the mess you left. What if I left you and took your son who you loved with all your heart? What if I sold the house out from under you? Imagine my selling your prized possessions and just gave you a few dollars. Think about how you would feel if after I took your son away and you called and I said to you Lil' Jack doesn't want to speak with you. You didn't even encourage him to talk to me. How would you feel with only a few days notice that you had to find a place to move to? How would you feel after serving me all those years to look up and see you had no one? When I was hungry Jack I learned to do without. I would just say to the Lord, "Lord let me use my hunger as an offering to you." I made it Jack by giving hunger as an offering to the one I love. And I didn't complain. Jack do you know how it feels to sleep on a cold hard floor and have no heat? I do and I survived because I was seeing a brighter day."

As I spoke I watched life leave Jack's face. I watched him go from standing to sitting down. I saw a look of pain come on this man that I loved all those years. I watched as his eyes turn red and tears fell from his eyes as I slowly spoke to him in love, truth and peace. There was an open conviction of power that hit this man. He even looked physically pained.

After about a few minutes of silence Jack stood up and came closer to me and said:

"I hate the man that beat you down
to the ground and stepped on you.
I always prided myself because I never hit
a woman physically. But I believe
that the greater pain is to destroy the spirit
of the woman.
I did all that and more.
I was unfaithful to you in so many ways.
I beat you everyday with my actions."

Jack broke into sobs and said. "Dear God I am sorry!" Something was breaking in this man right in front of my eyes. I saw his shoulders slump and I said, "Jack I have forgiven you for all that you did to me. I died but I have been resurrected to a new life with Jesus Christ."

23

The Manifestation

Before Jack left out the door he said that, "I can't help where I've been. But I can change where I am going. Perhaps I'll call on this God you serve who gave you the power to forgive me, to help me. Then I can forgive myself for treating you as less than that puppy that I stepped on."

Three weeks later on the way to my apartment I checked the mail and I got the shock of my lifetime. There was a check for more than enough money to open up another restaurant if we were careful.

My parent's estate had been settled and there was a policy to be cashed in with my name on it for fifty thousand dollar for me since I didn't go to college. My parents never cashed it in. I fought back the tears as I called my sister Marlo. She was so happy for me. We were becoming fast friends and looking forward to a reunion soon.

I called Jack Jr. and he was so excited. This meant we could put a payment on this building that we had checked out. It was perfect for what we wanted. Of course we got the building with no struggle. Friends came from all over. Before long we had a beautiful big shell painted creamy white and lemon yellow.

Jack Sr. suggested that we put up big screens all around the restaurant and get videos of salt water fish. And we could show videos of different places throughout the world where people have not been able to travel and they could visit there as a family. And that on that day when a video of a certain place was being shown we would prepare food representing that particular country or location. It was a great idea!

Jack is a changed man.

A year ago he came and said out of all that he has done in his life nothing had brought him any real peace. He pointed out the peace and contentment that Jack Jr. and I have and said that he wished that he could have that same peace. I said, "Jack you can." That night Jack received Jesus. I have never seen such a beautiful transformation and such a change in a human being.

We have become really good friends. Just the other day Jack gave me a check for one-hundred thousand dollars. I told Jack that I couldn't except it, and Jack Jr. said, "Mom take it, dad has made a lot of money off investments over the years." Jack Sr. said, "Jo, it's yours with no strings attached. The money that I invested was yours also." He didn't have to offer it to me twice.

The first thing that I did was give my tithes and offering unto the Lord as I always do. This is one reason why I believe that I am blessed. I put some money in Jack Jr.'s savings.

Next, I gave the workers that had been with me for a good season at least a one-thousand-dollar bonus if not more. Each worker was encouraged to go the bank and put some of the money into an account. Jack takes time out to teach all the workers about investing for the future.

Whatever we learn to help us in life as we continue to build, I want those who labor along with me to go up with us. Bye the way Mrs. Morgan has moved and has a beautiful place. She is now the overseer of "The Place of De´Light" in each of the major Josiephine De´Light Restaurants. She has taken to flying like a bird in the air.

Sarah accompanies her to make sure the breads are up to company standards and they love what they do. The sisters have of course expanded to other cities with the hat shops and each store has the same peace in the air.

24

The Long Way Around

Long ago as a young woman fresh out of high school, I made choices that cost me years and years in the wilderness. I know by my own actions that I stayed longer than I should have stayed. I took the long way around because I was satisfied with what I had. I never aimed higher. Never questioned whether life had anything better to offer.

Day after day and year after year I wondered in the wilderness. I should have known that if I was seeing the same scenery that something was wrong. I never questioned what I was born for. I suppressed every dream and told myself that I was already home. I've had some hard days and some angry nights. I lost myself along the way not knowing who I was. I had patterned myself after someone else's blueprint for my life. And then when they were fed up with the flavor I brought to the table I was dropped like a hot potato. When I was dropped I was picked up by someone and given a road map that has charted my course. The compass stayed on peace as long as I stayed on course. When I got off course the compass changed to let me know that I was off course. I traveled down some streets that I didn't have to travel. Streets of pain and avenues of unrest, lanes of mockery, places of rejection, hills of loneliness, days of over eating, steps of no anticipation, dead ends of neglect to self, a forest of being used and taken for granted. Valley's of shame. A freeway of slavery, And not to mentioned the mountains of not being valued are just a few of the places that I've traveled.

Dreamless years passed! Visionless days passed! I went through hopeless valley. Oh! But one day I saw a great light and was led to the place that I was destined to be. I am at a place in life now that I am the owner of restaurant franchises all over the world. Yes, I do have a dream home. Also several homes for the homeless and the color schemes are the same as the restaurants. We are opening homes for the elderly now. These homes are for the ones that may have missed the boat and their strength has gone. But I wanted them to experience being home in an atmosphere of peace.

We also do travel tours at low cost for those who may have never gotten the opportunity to travel and see the sites of beauty all over the world.

I stay so busy that I have never gained any of the weight back that I lost. I stay locked in at a particular place. I still have my hand cream until this day and I keep my hands moisturized, and I also still have the face cream. Now I can afford to have a manicure and a facial as often as I desire to.

I am on my way to becoming a billionaire. I still have my peace so I know that I am on the right track. I took the long way around but I made it.

By the way I am engaged to be married to Mr. Jack De´Light in three months!

COMING ATTRACTIONS…

Look For!

THE LONG WAY AROUND TEXT BOOK

By Veronica L. Bea and Vikki Freeman

Yes! A text book on the story of *The Long Way Around*!

Lets explore chapter by chapter and trace the life of Josiephine De´Light and her family.

We are sure to find <u>hidden</u> treasure!

Josiephine experienced rejection and it took her some places and locked her in.

WHAT ABOUT YOU?

Josiephine was looking for acceptance…She had family problems…She was asleep for years…She spent her life trying to please

Josiephine's world was framed by the size of her <u>thinking</u>.

Let check out how we fit in this picture and what we can get out of it.

What about her husband and her child? What can we learn from this family?

Now get your Bible out and let's dig golden nuggets for our future!

WHAT AN EXCITING WAY TO STUDY THE BIBLE!

Let's study the Word of God!
Guaranteed to beat all odds!

THE LONG WAY AROUND DEVOTIONAL

By Veronica L. Bea

Read exciting poems like.

I'm Remembering
Woman of Prayer
The Big Spill
Who would Have Thought
Old Clothes Rack

Each poem is filled with golden nuggets with a 21th century flavor! Hear the word of God for you each time you read a line!

You'll Laugh

You'll Cry

Make it a family affair as you read!!!!

Read about Josiephine De´Light...who gave up her goods without a fight...Nothing in my life seem to work out right...etc.

A verse from the scriptures heads each poem!

It you are thirsty read and drink!

A New Day

By Veronica L. Bea

A prophetic poem for this day

Yes there is a word from the Lord wrapped up in the pages of this book!

"Listen"

I feel the breaking of a new day
God is moving in an unusual way
This is my day
I better listen to what He has to say…

…and much more

Carry this little book around with you to be reminded of the special word God has just for you!

As you read it allow the breath of God to breathe on you!!!

THE PROPHET IS LOOSE I

By Veronica L. Bea

Poems with a word from the Lord just for you!

"Stop living in the fast lane
Quit acting insane
One day you'll stand before me and you'll explain
Why are you treating life like a game
It's time for change
Come closer you are out of range"

THE PROPHET IS LOOSE II

More exciting poems with the word of the Lord just for you.

"You'll just have to open this book
Take a look
Read it while you cook
Next thing you know you'll be hooked"

Look for these exciting books in the days to come in your local book stores!

To Purchase Books

You may order directly from:

Vlbea Freedom
4008 Hamilton Avenue
Cincinnati, Ohio 45223

Phone: 513 542-0178

Enquire about other products:
Posters
Caps
Tee Shirts (with special poems)
Framed poems
Poems on CD
Poems on Cassette Tapes

Personalize with names can be done on some of the products!

Remember we Love All People!!!

See L.A.P. Plus Freedom
For men and women dress hats, casual caps and hats, etc.
Special bulk order T-Shirts
Ask about Jack DéLight speciality
phone 513-542-0178